THE 48 LAWS OF DIVINE POWER

THE 48 LAWS OF
DIVINE
POWER

DR. C. ERROL BALL

PRODUCTIONS

COPYRIGHT © 2026 DR. CURTIS ERROL BALL

All rights reserved. No portion of this book may be reproduced in any form without written permission from the publisher or author, except as permitted by US copyright law.

THE 48 LAWS OF DIVINE POWER

FIRST EDITION

ISBN 978-1-5445-5089-3 *Hardcover*
      978-1-5445-5088-6 *Paperback*
      978-1-5445-5090-9 *Ebook*

To God—my Creator, my Lord and Savior Jesus Christ, and the abiding presence of the Holy Spirit—this work is humbly dedicated.

Life itself is Your gift to us, and what we do with that life is our gift back to You.

I thank You for seeing in me what I could not see in myself—for calling me worthy when I felt unworthy, for valuing me when I felt valueless, for loving me steadfastly through my missteps.

In response to such unshakable love, I offer my body as a living sacrifice—my daily act of worship. This book is one expression of that sacrifice: a testimony of devotion, an offering of obedience. May I be Your ambassador, Your watchman, Your vessel— whatever You need me to be for this hour, this time, this era.

An era where itching ears prefer pulpit performance over the purity of the Word. Where philosophies of greed, manipulation, and power seek to drown out the call to love our neighbor. Yet in this present darkness, Your light pierces brightest through the night.

So I dedicate this book to You, O Lord, for Your glory and Your honor. For in You I live and move and have my being. By the sustaining power of the Holy Spirit, may this work guide others into the truth of Scripture.

I shall not bury the gifts and talents You have entrusted to me. I will use them, multiply them, and pour them out until I am no more.

Soli Deo Gloria (To God alone be the glory)

CONTENTS

INTRODUCTION 9

PART I: THE FOUNDATION OF DIVINE POWER
1. DIVINE POWER BEGINS IN WEAKNESS 19
2. HUMILITY IS HEAVEN'S HEADQUARTERS 23
3. SILENCE IS A SACRED STRATEGY 27
4. PURPOSE PRECEDES PLATFORM 31
5. WAITING IS A WEAPON 35
6. BROKENNESS BUILDS BOLDNESS 39
7. CHARACTER QUALIFIES THE CALLED 43
8. OBEDIENCE OUTWEIGHS OUTCOMES 47
9. CONSECRATION CANCELS COUNTERFEITS 53
10. REVELATION PRECEDES RELEASE 57
11. IDENTITY OVER IMAGE 59
12. REPENTANCE RESURRECTS POWER 63
13. THE SECRET PLACE SECURES PUBLIC POWER 69
14. GRATITUDE GATHERS GRACE 73
15. INTIMACY WITH GOD IS THE HIGHEST INFLUENCE 77
16. FAITH FRAMES YOUR FUTURE 81
17. REJECTION IS DIVINE REDIRECTION 85
18. THE WORD IS YOUR WEAPON 89
    PART I SUMMARY 93

PART II: THE FUNCTION OF DIVINE POWER
19. SERVING UNLOCKS SUPERNATURAL STRATEGY 99
20. DISCERNMENT GUIDES DOMINION 103
21. PEACE IS THE PROOF OF POWER 109
22. THE HOLY SPIRIT IS YOUR OPERATING SYSTEM 113
23. MIRACLES MOVE THROUGH MOVEMENT 117
24. INTEGRITY INVITES INCREASES 121
25. FASTING FUELS FUNCTION 125
26. UNITY MULTIPLIES POWER 129
27. FORGIVENESS FREES THE FLOW 133
28. JOY STABILIZES FUNCTION 137
29. EXCELLENCE EXPANDS AUTHORITY 143
30. COMPASSION IS DIVINE CURRENCY 147
31. TIMING TRUMPS TALENT 151
32. BLESSING FOLLOWS BOUNDARIES 155
33. LISTENING POSITIONS YOU FOR LAUNCH 159
34. HONOR ACTIVATES HEAVEN 163
35. REST IS A RENEWAL STRATEGY 167
36. GIVE GLORY OR LOSE GRACE 171
    PART II SUMMARY 175

PART III: THE FULLNESS OF DIVINE POWER
37. INHERITANCE IS RELEASED THROUGH INTIMACY 181
38. MULTIPLICATION IS THE MARK OF DIVINE POWER 185
39. MANTLES ARE FOR MOVEMENT 189
40. AUTHORITY REQUIRES ACCOUNTABILITY 193
41. STEWARDSHIP SUSTAINS SUPPLY 197
42. WHOLENESS PRECEDES WITNESS 201
43. WITNESS IS A WEAPON 205
44. LEGACY IS GREATER THAN LOYALTY TO SELF 209
45. POWER FLOWS TO THE POURED OUT 213
46. THE POWER OF LOVE 217
47. GLORY WITHOUT GOD IS GRAVEYARD DUST 221
48. FULLNESS IS FOUND IN FINISHING WELL 225
    PART III SUMMARY 229

    CONCLUSION 231
    ACKNOWLEDGMENTS 235
    ABOUT THE AUTHOR 239

INTRODUCTION

Power Reclaimed

I have watched, in both my ministry and my medical practice, what people reach for when life presses in on them. I don't come to you as one untouched by the pull of the world's philosophies. I come as one who has seen, up close, what happens when hearts hungry for hope turn to hollow sources.

As a physician, I've seen patients in the waiting room—anxious, depressed—flipping frantically through *The 48 Laws of Power* by Robert Greene as if the next page might hold their rescue.

I've been on airplanes, seated next to passengers who pulled it from their carry-on. When I've asked, "Do you like what you're reading?" they've replied, "Trying to…my friend swears by it, so I'm going to give it a try."

I've seen friends and family—people I've known for years—raised in loving, God-fearing homes, believers themselves, yet caught up in whatever is trending, willing to bend convictions to climb higher. Even believers, quietly re-wiring their minds away from the ancient wisdom of Proverbs 1:8 ("My son, hear the instruction of thy father, and forsake not the law of thy mother.") toward tactics their parents and pastors would never endorse: trickery, deception, calculated flattery. (Note: All biblical passages will be from the King James Version unless otherwise specified.)

And I have seen the toll.

Emotions frayed.

Minds weary.

Bodies exhausted.

Faith replaced by a counterfeit gospel—Robert Greene's "bible" of self over Savior.

Faith replaced by fabricated facades of deception and exploitation, which he teaches as a means of getting ahead and obtaining power, is a strategy of folly. There is no thought of being my brother's keeper, or of love or compassion for my fellow human being. Only a foolish thought that all others are mere objects to be exploited. Sadly, the foundation of this mindset is just as frail as the ones advocating it.

This is not just about what people read—it's about what people become.

Ideas shape souls. There is no darker deception than when a man calls evil effective and mislabels manipulation as mastery. For when exploitation begins to feel natural and deception starts to look divine, the conscience is seared and the soul corrodes. Fascination becomes formation, because what you tune into, you may end up turning into.

This is not me standing above you, wagging a finger. This is me, standing beside you, waving a hand and saying: "I've seen where that road leads…there's a better way."

I've watched too many reach for strategies that strip away

the very character God calls us to keep. That is why *The 48 Laws of Divine Power* exists—not to condemn, but to counter. To give you something better to reach for. To ground you in God's Word with clear, memorable truths that will calm your emotions, settle your mind, and strengthen your body for whatever comes.

I say with both compassion and conviction:

Lay aside the lure of manipulation.

Lay aside the false glamour of self-glory.

Lay aside Greene…and go after God.

Because there's a power that cannot be bought, broken, or bankrupted. A power that cleanses even as it calls you higher.

LAY ASIDE GREENE…GO AFTER GOD

Divine power isn't grasped. It's given. It isn't manipulated. It's manifested. It isn't about rising above others. It's about being raised by God.

The world teaches power as domination.

Heaven reveals it as a demonstration.

Robert Greene's *The 48 Laws of Power* has seduced millions with its seductive strategies of control, manipulation, and fear. But what if real power isn't taken—it's entrusted? What if the greatest authority isn't found in outsmarting others, but in out-surrendering them?

In this book, we break the spell of worldly influence and restore Heaven's framework for righteous leadership, victorious living, and supernatural influence. Each of these forty-eight laws is laced with fire from Scripture and examples from saints who wielded power not through deceit, but through devotion. And when necessary, we name names. We confront the Greene gospel of gain with the gold of God's Word.

A CALL TO THOSE WHO DESIRE MORE

What if you could access a power that moves mountains, splits seas, shuts the mouths of lions, raises the dead, and heals the sick?

What if that power was never meant to be rare, but regular—not reserved for the prophets of old, but released to the believers of today?

We live in a world obsessed with positional power—political, social, financial. But Heaven offers a different blueprint. A power that doesn't promote self—but reveals the Savior. A power that doesn't corrupt—but cleanses. That power is divine, and it belongs to those willing to lay down worldly weapons and pick up the mantle of God.

WHY THIS BOOK?

This book is a roadmap—a spiritual gridline—an unlocking of the forty-eight laws of divine power that govern the invisible realm and manifest in real results.

These laws are not human constructs—they are pulled from God's eternal Word, and proven through the lives of Moses, Esther, David, Daniel, Elijah, and ultimately, Jesus Christ Himself.

And while I am not a world-renowned theologian like William Barclay, James Cone, John C. Maxwell, Willie Jennings, or John MacArthur—I come to this table not with fame or celebrity, but with faithfulness.

Who am I? I accepted the call to ministry thirty-five years ago, and to medicine twenty years ago.

As a minister, I've buried the dead...

...and brought forth life as a physician.

I've seen hearts flatline...

...and seen the heartbroken revived through prayer and presence.

And in all of that, I've noticed something stunning in the human condition:

We always want more when our time feels like less.

We put off for tomorrow what Heaven is calling us to do today.

But today, if you hear His voice, harden not your heart.

I've stood at deathbeds and delivery rooms, in pulpits and emergency rooms, and I've seen this truth: we all must face tomorrow.

And the best way to face it...is with divine power.

DIVINE POWER VS. HUMAN POWER

Human power depends on resources, resumes, and reputation.

It can be purchased, politicized, and puffed up.

But divine power?

It's eternal, unstoppable, and available to all who are willing to humble themselves and walk in truth.

Human power says, "I must climb higher."

Divine power says if I be lifted up, I'll draw all men unto me.

HOW THIS BOOK IS ORGANIZED

We don't drop forty-eight laws on you like a firehose.

We guide you law by law, precept upon precept, and move you through three sacred phases:

PART I: FOUNDATION

This is where it all begins.

We unearth the pillars. We address the posture.

We expose the lies and lay the groundwork for the truth.

You'll learn that divine power begins not in strength—but in surrender.

You'll confront your false self and claim your true spiritual identity.

This part resets the soul's soil to receive God's seed.

PART II: FUNCTION

Here, divine power becomes a practice.

We show how to live it, move in it, multiply it, and manage it.

You'll discover that fasting fuels function, timing trumps talent, miracles move through movement, and integrity invites increase.

This section is where the theory becomes testimony. Where faith becomes fruition.

PART III: FULLNESS

This is the high place. The summit.

Not perfection—but completion in Christ.

Here, we reveal that mantles are for movement, authority demands accountability, power must be poured out, and wholeness precedes witness.

The journey leads to the ultimate truth: fullness is not found in accolades, but in finishing well.

This book will teach you to:

- Tap into the authority of your faith
- Operate in discernment and obedience
- Walk through spiritual warfare without weariness

- Steward your mantle with purpose
- Pour out your oil with precision
- Finish your assignment full of fire and faith

Now turn the page, and prepare to encounter the kind of power that cannot be explained—only experienced.

A power that lives in you, flows through you, and points back to the only One who gets the glory.

This is divine power.

And this…is your time.

PART I

THE FOUNDATION OF DIVINE POWER

Robert Greene, author of *The 48 Laws of Power*, builds his foundation on the idea that power is amoral, competitive, and essential for survival. In his introduction he openly admits, "Power is a game, and in games you do not judge your opponents by their intentions but by the effects of their actions."

True power is not a game, it's a gift. While Greene's foundation is built on fear, cunning, and suspicion, the foundation of divine power is faith, truth, and wisdom. A God-given foundation is not about manipulating perception but manifesting purpose.

Before you build tall, you must dig deep. Before you garner strength, you must garden-ready soil. Robert Greene offers sandcastles—slick, seductive strategies rooted in fear, falsehood, and flesh. His power is indeed a game, and he wants you to play it with a poker face and poisonous tongue.

But divine power isn't a game. It's a government. It's not temporary tactics but timeless truth.

Greene's gospel is Machiavelli's memoir with a modern remix. He suggests you must either manipulate or be manipulated. Hide your hand. Mask your motives. Be feared more than loved.

But God says, "The fear of the Lord is the beginning of wisdom: and the knowledge of the holy is understanding" (Proverbs 9:10). Not fear of man. Not fear of missing out. Not power for applause but power for assignment.

You don't build a kingdom on cunning. You build it on covenant.

Let this be your foundation: Not strategy, but surrender. Not deceit, but divine design. Not winning the game, but walking in godly governance. This is not about rising to the top; this is about starting at the Rock.

LAW 1

DIVINE POWER BEGINS IN WEAKNESS

"...My grace is sufficient for thee: for my strength is made perfect in weakness..."

—2 CORINTHIANS 12:9

So, you're wondering why the room always seems to shrink when you walk in. Why you're skipped, sidelined, and slighted—passed over for the promotion, ignored in the meeting, ghosted by the one you prayed might finally see you. You think they counted you out? Even better—God counts differently. Their rejection was divine redirection. Their silence was sacred stillness. You thought they saw your flaws? Good. Because God saw them first—and still chose you.

The divine doesn't search for dominance—it looks for dependency. It's not your strength that attracts Heaven, it's your surrender. Divine power doesn't debut in glory. It grows in the gutters. It's conceived in chaos, matured in obscurity, and birthed in brokenness. While men measure resumes, God measures readiness. While others demand pedigree, God searches for pliability. He's not impressed by crowns; He's drawn to cracks. Because in every cracked vessel, glory can leak out.

Let's talk Moses. A misfit from the moment he was born—hidden, floated, forgotten. The Nile became his nursery, and abandonment his adoption. Can you imagine being placed in a basket, surrounded by serpents, crocodiles, and currents that could've crushed him? His first breath of favor came not from family, but from Pharaoh's palace—proof that providence outruns pedigree.

He grew up caught between two worlds—Egyptian in appearance, Hebrew in blood. Culture confused his calling. When he opened his mouth, he stammered—because his tongue trembled with trauma. Shame shaped his speech. He tried to cover up his culture, mask his memories, and downplay his differences. He didn't stutter because he lacked vocabulary—he stuttered because he lacked validation.

Yet, this is the one God chose. The one who couldn't complete a sentence without stumbling. The one who questioned his worth with every word. God didn't call the eloquent. He called the insecure. Because divine power prefers a partner who knows his limits. The bush burned and the call came—not when Moses was mighty, but when he was meager. Not when he had Pharaoh's favor, but when he was herding sheep in the shadows.

Now the scene shifts to Gideon. Hiding in a winepress—threshing wheat in secret. Fearful. Frustrated. Forgotten. His environment screamed oppression. His spirit echoed depression. He called himself the least of the least—God called him "mighty man of valor." Heaven speaks in contradiction. God often names you by your destiny before you can detach from your dysfunction.

Gideon had trust issues—not just with people, but with providence. He needed proof, not because he was petty, but because he was petrified. He didn't see a warrior in the mirror—he saw a worrier. And still, God trusted him before Gideon could trust himself. He didn't wait for perfect faith—He moved on trembling obedience.

Let that settle: It wasn't Gideon's might. It was his motion. Not his courage—but his compliance. Just enough yes to trigger divine power. Heaven doesn't require fearlessness, only faithfulness. Rather than be paralyzed in fear—even though being honest he was transparently afraid—yet, trembling, he still moved forward in spite of his fear. His "act" of obedience… like a soldier, getting an order to "move" forward…forward march. That's what Gideon did. He got his marching papers, and although he didn't see himself as "marching material," he acted on faith. He moved.

Jesus says in Matthew 17:20, "And Jesus said unto them, Because of your unbelief: for verily I say unto you, if ye have faith as a grain of mustard seed, ye shall say unto this mountain, remove hence to yonder place; and it shall remove; and nothing shall be impossible unto you." Gideon is that verse personified: a person with little faith, but it doesn't take much to become a mighty man of valor. A mustard seed of movement can overturn mountains of mediocrity.

Divine power doesn't ignore weakness—it inhabits it. Scripture doesn't sanitize saints—it showcases their scars. Paul's thorn was never removed. Timothy's timidity wasn't rebuked. Peter's denial became his destiny. Why? Because power made perfect in perfection glorifies man. But power made perfect in weakness glorifies God.

Weakness isn't a liability. It's a ladder. A holy invitation for Heaven to descend. When you feel too flawed, too fractured, too far gone—you're the perfect candidate for divine demonstration. In the Kingdom, lowliness is leverage, and insufficiency is sacred space.

So, what about you? You, with the doubt. You, with the disjointed dreams. You, with the trembling hands and the haunted past. Hear this: God doesn't need your perfection. He needs your participation.

One trembling step at a time. One hesitant yes after another. And before you know it, divine power will flow—not because you're strong, but because you stayed. Not because you arrived, but because you were available. He doesn't anoint the arrogant. He empowers the emptied.

So, stand—stammering if you must. Obey—afraid if you must. Walk—limping if you must. Because in your weakness, God writes wonders. And in your lack, Heaven looses limitless power.

LAW 2

HUMILITY IS HEAVEN'S HEADQUARTERS

"Humble yourselves therefore under the mighty hand of God, that he may exalt you in due time."

—1 PETER 5:6

You want to go high? We all do. The corner office. The center mic. The verified badge. The applause, the access, the accolades. But Heaven doesn't hand out power based on popularity. God doesn't elevate egos—He exalts the emptied.

The way up is still down. The crown still comes after the cross.

In this kingdom, the escalator to excellence is humility. Not the fake, performative humility that posts itself. Not the kind that bends the knee for likes. No—the sacred posture of one who bows low not to be seen, but to serve.

Why is humility Heaven's headquarters? Because pride pollutes the presence of God. Pride is a parasite. It siphons glory from the Giver and feeds it to the flesh. And make no mistake—where pride resides, power hides.

Lucifer lost his place—not for lack of gifting, but for lusting after God's glory. Nebuchadnezzar lost his mind—not for poor leadership, but for praising himself.

Pharaoh hardened his heart—and Heaven humbled him with plagues.

Pride is not just a personality flaw. It's a spiritual felony. It's a crime against the Creator's supremacy.

But humility? Humility is Heaven's calling card. It tells God, "I trust You with my timing. I yield to Your yoke. I submit to Your script. I will not demand what You haven't delivered."

Humility is not weakness. It's willingness. Not hiding—but yielding. Not thinking less of yourself, but thinking of yourself less.

Remember Joseph? Not just the governor of Egypt, but the graduate of God's school of humility. God gave him a dream—divine, dazzling, destiny-soaked. But Joseph made one mistake: he shared it too soon, too loud, too proud. And when divine dreams are announced in immature voices, they sound like arrogance.

Joseph told of the dream—but God had to teach him to steward it. Because it's one thing to receive revelation. It's another to be refined for responsibility.

From the pit to Potiphar's house. From Potiphar's house to prison. From prison to the palace. Every promotion was preceded by humiliation. Every door God opened came after Joseph bowed low in suffering.

What felt like back-to-back betrayal was actually a step-by-step boot camp. He wasn't cursed, he was being conditioned. Not demoted but developed.

And when Pharaoh needed a dream decoded, Joseph didn't stand tall—he stood surrendered. He didn't say, "I have the power," but instead said, "God shall give Pharaoh an answer of peace" (Genesis 41:16).

That's the shift. That's the spiritual success. When your gift no longer fuels your ego, but funnels God's glory.

The world says, "Stand up and be seen." Heaven says, "Kneel down and be sent."

The world says, "Be your own boss." God says, "Be My bondservant."

The fastest way to forfeit divine favor is to believe you built it yourself. Divine power flows downhill. Always. It seeks the lowest place, the yielded space, the surrendered soul.

So, check your posture. Are you low enough for God to lift you? Because if you climb too high without Him, He'll humble you before the crowd. But if you bow before Him in secret, He'll exalt you in public places your feet never earned.

God doesn't give platforms to those who crave applause more than assignment. He doesn't promote people who treat power like a prop. Humility is His hedge against self-destruction.

When you feel like life is pressing you, pruning you, paining you—it's not bad luck. It's sacred training. Spiritual resistance training. Boot camp for the blessed. Because when the blessing comes, pride must not be seated at the table. Only grace. Only gratitude. Only God.

He gives grace to the humble. He promotes those who posture their hearts downward. Not to grovel but to grow. Not to shrink but to shine under His glory.

So, if you want to go high—start low. Not with ambition, but with submission. Not with branding, but with bending. Not with demand, but with devotion.

Bow before you build. Surrender before you strategize. Repent before you rise.

Because Heaven does not reside in the lofty. It reigns in the lowly. Humility is not just the hallway to divine power—it's the headquarters.

LAW 3

SILENCE IS A SACRED STRATEGY

"Even a fool, when he holdeth his peace, is counted wise: and he that shutteth his lips is esteemed a man of understanding."

—PROVERBS 17:28

The world will tell you to "promote yourself." God says, "Be still and know that I am God (Psalm 46:10). Sometimes the most powerful move you can make, the best flex, is to say nothing at all. Did you catch that? Well, once more then: the best flex is sometimes to say nothing at all.

Silence isn't weakness. It's warfare. It's the strategy of the strong who know that volume doesn't verify value. Jesus didn't speak in front of Herod. Joseph learned not to share his dreams with his brothers any longer. Mary treasured what she saw in her heart. He that guards his tongue governs his tomorrow.

Robert Greene teaches you to court attention. But God

teaches you to cultivate anointing. And anointing grows best in quiet gardens, not public stages.

You don't have to explain everything. You don't have to post everything. You don't have to prove anything. Just let your silence become your sanctuary. But stay silent and let God speak on your behalf while you stay hidden in Him.

Remember, some strength only develops in silence. Power that talks too much, leaks. And when you leak, when your time to explode onto the scene arrives, your impact becomes a dud. And it's because you blew out just as soon as you blew up.

He that guards his tongue governs his tomorrow.

There's holiness in the quiet. There's glory in the grip of the guarded. There's strength in the still. Not every thought needs a microphone. Not every vision needs validation. Some desires are divine deposits, not meant for discussion but for devotion.

So, guard your heart, the good Word warns in Proverbs 4:23, for out of it flows the issues of life. Don't let loose what hasn't been laid down at the Lord's feet. The crowd, the naysayers, the co-workers, your circle, etc., won't always understand it. They don't need to. That dream? That deep thing inside? It's not for display. It's for divine development, then deployment. The Bible says there's a time to speak and a time to stay silent. That means the timing of the Word is just as sacred as the truth of the Word because what goes out can't come back in. Once it flies from the lips, it forms life…or it ignites loss. So, wait. Weight it. Worship while you hold it, because speaking too soon can sink a season. A reckless tongue starts wars, but a restrained and silent tongue saves us from them.

This is not passivity. This is prophetic discipline. This is not cowardice. This is consecrated control. When you master your mouth, you manifest divine maturity. To say nothing when your flesh wants to clap back and shout is not weakness. It is wisdom. It is engaged spiritual warfare. It is power divine.

The lesson of the day: Keep it sacred. Keep it still. Keep it silent. Heaven hears if you must share, and Heaven won't share it until it's ready to rain down from Heaven the great and wonderful things God is doing in your life. Until then, just being able to hush takes power and strength. In fact, it's power held in check.

LAW 4

PURPOSE PRECEDES PLATFORM

"There are many devices in a man's heart; nevertheless, the counsel of the Lord, that shall stand."

—PROVERBS 19:21

In a world where everyone's building a brand, few are building on bedrock. We're flooded with feeds but famished for a solid foundation. Most influencers and platform seekers want the mic but reject the mandate. They chase influence, but ignore the inner work. But let it be declared: Divine power doesn't follow followers. It follows faithfulness to purpose.

Before the lights, before the likes, before the livestream—God looks for lives aligned with His assignment. Not clout. Not charisma. But calling. And calling that's been cultivated and consecrated in secret. Because in the Kingdom, the spotlight is sacred, and only purpose has the weight to hold it without breaking.

Know this: God never anoints what He doesn't appoint. And He never appoints what He hasn't prepared. This divine order can't be skipped, swiped through, or sped up by savvy marketing. Purpose is the prerequisite for platform. And until that is settled, your stage will betray you.

From Genesis to Revelation, we see a God who works from depth before display, who forms before He fills, who conceals before He reveals. Adam was shaped before he was shown. Moses was called before he was commissioned. David was crowned in secret before he ever set foot in the palace.

Purpose is not performance. It's not a TED Talk with a tinge of theology. It's not a perfectly cropped sermon clip. It's not hustle baptized in Christianese. Purpose is a divine assignment etched into your essence. It predates platforms and outlasts applause.

We are living in the age of clout without calling. Digital dopamine versus divine deployment. Podcast pulpits. Instagram intercessors. AI-authored anointings. Greene says, "Fake it 'til you make it." But divine power says, "Wait until He breaks it."

Why? Because what God doesn't break, He can't truly bless. What hasn't been humbled can't be held up. And if your stage is stronger than your soul, you will collapse under the crowd you begged for.

Let's not be fooled by fast growth and flashy graphics. The Kingdom does not operate on algorithms. It operates on alignment.

David was anointed in obscurity—then sent back to serve sheep. He wasn't trending. He wasn't performing. He was practicing with slings and songs when nobody was watching.

Joseph had dreams of dominion—but God dragged him through dungeons before He delivered him to Pharaoh's palace. Why? Because the platform he was destined for required emotional maturity, spiritual security, and divine dependency.

Even Jesus—the spotless Son of God—spent thirty years in silence before stepping into three years of ministry. He who had all authority waited. Why? Because purpose must be proven in private before power is public.

Here's the nonnegotiable, Heaven-endorsed truth that is irrefutable: the platform must sit on purpose—or it will sink under pressure.

- Before you build, test the bedrock.
- Before you preach, know the pattern.
- Before you post, be planted.

Sand feels stable in summer. But when storms hit—only the rock will remain.

Jesus said it: the wise man builds on the Rock. Not the reaction. Not the retweets. Not the reach. The Rock. The revelation. The root system that doesn't shout—but survives.

Let the world chase stages. Let them gather microphones and magazine covers. Let them decorate sandcastles and do laps for likes.

But you? Chase submission. Chase silence over spotlight. Surrender over sensation. Dig deep. Build slow. Let God be the Architect. Because what He builds can't be broken. What He calls can't be cancelled.

And when the winds howl, the critics speak, the spotlight fades, and the season shifts—you will still be standing. Not because of platform. But because of purpose—planted in the Rock, prepared in the dark, and powered by the Divine.

LAW 5

WAITING IS A WEAPON

"But they that wait upon the LORD shall renew their strength; they shall mount up with wings as eagles…"

—ISAIAH 40:31

We live in a world that wants in, now. Greene says, "Seize the moment. Force the hand. Control the clock." But divine power knows that timing is everything. Waiting isn't passive, it's prophetic. It's Heaven's reminder that your blessing has a schedule.

Ask Abraham. He got weary of waiting for Sarah to bring him Isaac and ended up with Ishmael via the housemaid, Hagar. The family tension that ensued afterwards became so much that Hagar and Ishmael were kicked out and made homeless. What if he had waited?

Waiting goes against the mindset of the majority of people around you who want everything, right now. The old guard who upheld virtuous principles like "Rome wasn't built in a day" have all died off and have been replaced with some modern day thinkers who would say, "Yeah it wasn't built in a day, and still eventually fell and was conquered by another, so might as well get it now and get it quickly, because in the end it will still fall just the same."

I dare say it takes more courage and strength and power to wait. To wait is to war against your own impatience. It is to tell your flesh, "You don't run this." It's to tell God, "I trust you even when I can't trace you or know your next move." Waiting is when the weak get weary and the wise get woven into His will.

Do not abort the assignment just because the clock is ticking loudly in your head. Power that moves outside of God's calendar always creates complications and will cause you to take a longer road to get back on the trail to your destination. Haste really does make for waste. A waste of time, energy, and often money and finances. So, stay with it and let your time be your time, and know when that time is not now. And those who wait? They have renewed strength. They mount up on wings of an eagle. They run and do not get weary. They walk and do not grow faint (Isaiah 40:31).

Maintain the power by not getting ahead of God. Remember the analogy of a shepherd, as described in Psalm 23, The Lord is my shepherd... We follow the shepherd's lead; we are behind Him, not in front of Him. Why? The shepherd won't lead us into danger, but leads us to still and calm waters, not turbulent, drowning waters. He leads us down the path of righteousness.

At times, He makes us lie down, as in *wait*. Not to be mean or to punish us. He makes us lie down in green pastures. Why? Because we sometimes get physically, emotionally, and spiritually weak when walking in His power. He makes us lie down and rest so we can get nourishment from the green pastures. So, He can restore our souls.

And why does our soul need strengthening? So that during those moments when we are walking through the valleys of life and the shadows of death are upon us, we will not fear evil, but instead have comfort. In those moments, our cup runs over as goodness (grace), and mercy follows us from behind.

So, why would you ever want to get too far from grace and mercy? Why would you ever move away from those who catch you if you stumble and fall backwards? And why would you ever want to get ahead of the shepherd who has ordered your steps?

Waiting is not only your power. It is your protective weapon against those who don't mean you well. So, continue to walk with God and keep things well with your soul.

LAW 6

BROKENNESS BUILDS BOLDNESS

"And not only so, but we glory in tribulations also: knowing that tribulation worketh patience; and patience, experience, and experience, hope: and hope maketh not ashamed…"

—ROMANS 5:3–5

Nobody wants to be broken. But everybody wants to be bold. We want the lion's roar without the lonely nights. The public courage without the private crushing. But divine power doesn't come dressed in comfort—it comes drenched in crushing.

Before God gives you a voice to shake the nations, He gives you a moment that shatters your assumptions. Before He gives you thunder in your testimony, He sends storms that test your trust. You want divine boldness? Then don't despise the divine breaking.

Romans 5 lays the blueprint: Suffering produces endurance. Endurance refines character. Character births hope. And hope rooted in Christ never, ever disappoints.

This is not just poetry—it's process. It's God's divine developmental system. Because character can't be microwaved. It must be marinated in trials. Hope isn't inherited—it's hammered into the heart through hardship.

He doesn't use the uncracked, the untouched, or the overly curated. He uses those who've been split open by sorrow and still remain in love with their Savior. Your brokenness is not a liability. It's divine leverage.

Look at Peter, a man who went from denial to dominion. Bold at first glance, but brittle beneath the surface. He declared loyalty with his lips, but denied Jesus with his life—not once, not twice, but three times. And then came the rooster, and then came the tears.

Fast forward—Peter's eyes lock with the risen Lord. No condemnation. Just a question, repeated three times like a salve to his soul: do you love me?

Each failure, met with grace. Each shame, swallowed by mercy. And then came the call from Jesus: feed my sheep. Feed them not because you're flawless—but because you're faithful now. Your brokenness has birthed boldness. Your failure has formed fearlessness. Your fracture has fashioned fire.

Haven't you been there? You knew what was right, but chose what was wrong. You made the move, sent the text, burned the bridge. And afterward, you looked in the mirror and said, "This ain't me."

But that's the exact place where Heaven meets humanity. That's where power is poured—not on the pedestal, but on the pavement of repentance.

God doesn't waste a wound. He doesn't discard the crushed. Instead, "The Lord is nigh unto them that are of a broken heart; and saveth such as be of a contrite spirit" (Psalm 34:18). He recycles regret into a reservoir of revelation.

What felt like the end was really the excavation—of buried gold, of dormant grit, of divine dependence. Your tears watered the soil of your next testimony. Your trauma tilled the ground for a deeper truth. And now, you don't just survive—you stand. Unshaken. Unbothered. Unapologetically appointed.

Let Greene and the world tell you: "Never show weakness." But our Gospel says: in weakness, Christ is revealed. Our brokenness is the backstage for divine brilliance. So, when you are:

- troubled on every side—but not crushed;
- perplexed—but not in despair;
- persecuted—but never forsaken; and
- cast down—but not destroyed (2 Corinthians 4–8),

you carry something unbreakable because you've been broken.

You are not fragile. You are forged. You are not ruined. You are refined. Your soul has survived the fire, and now it shines with a strength not your own.

So don't curse the crushing. Don't resist the refining. Your breaking was the birthplace of your boldness. Your losses became your leverage. Your weakness became your weapon.

Let the winds blow, the waves rise, and the whispers of the past try to haunt you. You've been through too much to turn back now. You've endured too long to question who walks with you. And when others see the boldness in your stride and the fire in your faith—they'll wonder where it came from.

And you'll say: it was built…in the breaking.

LAW 7

CHARACTER QUALIFIES THE CALLED

"He that is faithful in that which is least is faithful also in much: and he that is unjust in the least will be unjust also in much."

—LUKE 16:10

You can be called. You can be gifted. You can be brilliant and bold and born for greatness. But if your character is cracked, your calling will collapse. While Greene says cultivate charm, God says cultivate character. Why? Because charisma might get you in the room, but character determines whether you'll stay in the room.

Joseph passed the palace test because he first passed the prison test. David spared King Saul's life not once but twice, because integrity outweighed his ambition.

Your power must match your purity. God is holy. The vessels

He fills must be as well. Don't just ask God to use you if you are not willing to also ask Him to refine you, restrain you, and rebuild you. And sometimes, to rebuild something that will last, you must first tear down, start from the foundation, and build back up.

God wants you to know that when, not if, the storm hits, it's not your gift that keeps you grounded; it's your guts, your grit, your grace, and your godliness. Because the higher your anointing, the deeper the accountability. Just know that if you truly want to carry something sacred and leave a legacy that lasts, let God chisel away what's still stubborn, because power without purity is a ticking time bomb. Being a person with character keeps it from blowing up your destiny, not to mention the collateral damage of hurting those close to you.

Remember, it's not your gift that guarantees God's go-ahead. It's your grit in the gap, your godliness in the gray, your grace in the garden where no one sees you pray. No one wants to hear you tell them how you shine in the spotlight; show them how you stand in the shadows. Don't brag about the platforms you speak from. Tell them about the promises you have kept when no one's peeking.

Character ain't cosmetic. It's core, carved, and consecrated. It's how you handle temptation without a timeline, treasure without a title, and tension without a tantrum. It is what you do when the crowd has cleared, the cameras cut, and you're left with nothing but your conscience and your calling. Because charisma can crack, but character carries you through. Charisma can draw a crowd, but character determines if great assembly of forerunners remains. Charisma often gets the mic, but character gets the mic and the mantle.

A man of character doesn't just talk truth, he treads it. He doesn't just quote Scripture, he walks it—even when it's costly.

He doesn't just live right when it's popular, he lives holy when it's painful, private, and prolonged. It's soothing for someone to look at you and say, if he is righteous in the limelight, he'll still be loyal in the lonely night. If she's honest on the mountaintop, she will still be holy when she is hurting in the valley. Because real power ain't in performance. It's in the proof of private purity.

So please, don't ask God to use you publicly if you won't let Him form you privately. Before you carry divine power, make sure your character can support the weight.

LAW 8

OBEDIENCE OUTWEIGHS OUTCOMES

"...to obey is better than sacrifice, and to hearken than the fat of rams."
—I SAMUEL 15:22

Many people believe that obedience is only validated by visible results. But in the Kingdom, results follow reverence. We often want to control and make power moves over others to sharpen our leadership skills—so we think.

Aristotle said it well with, "He who has never learned to obey cannot be a good commander."

Noah obeyed without rain. In fact, there had been no mention of rain beforehand. He obeyed without fully understanding what would happen next. He just knew he was supposed to build an ark. Despite being laughed at, hearing people say, "What in the hell is this fool doing?" he continued to build.

Perhaps they thought he was consumed with old wine and a bit intoxicated. Nevertheless, he didn't fold. He just obeyed.

Abraham obeyed without knowing the destination. While he had a vision, the vision was not a clear picture of a destination. The vision sometimes is to get up and walk with God, and that was good enough for Abraham. He found out the destination when he got there. He believed and trusted that God would guide him.

In your life's situation, sometimes you want to see the end. Well, have you ever gotten into your car to drive to another city or state? Do you have to see that state or city before you get in your car, fill up the gas tank, grab a few snacks, and get on the highway? The answer is obvious: you do not. In fact, you don't even know if there is going to be road construction or detours. One thing is certain: regardless of potential delays, you are going to another state for something that's not present where you are. If that were the case, there would be no need to travel. God understands this common sense perfectly, because He gave it to you.

When God presses a vision upon you to get up and go, and you hesitate or procrastinate—even though you know without a doubt it was God through the Holy Spirit telling you it's time to leave that company of friends, that job, and start afresh—after a few days, that strong urge to make changes will leave. You might assume it was just a temporary emotion. But God saw that you were not as ready as you thought to possess the power to make moves when no one else is in motion. So, the vision vanished due to a lack of obedience. Many times we want change but do not want to acknowledge that the change begins with us. We want better, but we sometimes have to let go of the good in order to get there. You cannot expect friends, family, and partners to understand. If they do, that's great; and if they don't, that has to be great too. Trust God for the result.

Obedience doesn't always feel productive. It often feels lonely, too slow for results, and sacrificial of time, relationships, and living. But it's the only soil where divine power takes root. Let the fruit come when it's time. Let the reward come in its season.

In Samuel 15, God gave Saul a clear command to destroy the Amalekites and every living thing. This wasn't impulsive wrath, but wrath delayed for centuries in response to the Amalekites' behaviors. They had a generational spirit of hostility and unrighteousness. As we delve deeper into this story, I want you to think of your family of origin. What ugly things go on and seem to show up in every generation? The family as a whole has normalized it, but the redeemed in the family see it for what it is: a generational curse. Then, I want you to ask yourself honestly, what is it that God has been pressing upon you—in your mind, your spirit—to say, to confront, to break the generational curse, to stop the cycle, and to heal? But you only go halfway. You are obedient to a point, but then you think about the rejection: no more invites to family events, the names you'll be called, made out to be the black sheep, and told you should have left well enough alone. Consider this: would God have put that burden on you if He didn't believe you could carry it?

God's command to Saul required obedience. He wasn't just clearing land, He was cleaning up a lineage. He wasn't just dealing with the enemy, He was sending a message about sin, subtlety, and selective obedience.

King Saul spared the king of Amalek. He also decided not to kill the good and healthy-looking livestock. He thought these animals were a good sacrifice he could make to God. He spared the king because he wanted a trophy, a bargaining chip. He tried to get ahead of God, and outran His grace. At his core, Saul wanted to make himself look good. "Hey, everyone, look what I did," as he shows off the king, now his captive. Perhaps he didn't want the blowback of the Israelites asking, "Why did you kill the cattle?" But selective obedience is still disobedience. God wasn't looking for modification; he was looking for submission. We don't get to edit God's instructions. Not fully obeying God is something we must all purge from ourselves.

Standing in our way is the desire to exalt ourselves instead of allowing God to exalt us. After the battle, Saul built an altar for himself, not to honor God as was the custom, but for himself. He later confessed that he hadn't fully obeyed because he didn't want the troops to be angry with him. He wanted to please men more than he did God.

Think again about your own situation. God desires to break the cycle of generational curses within your family. But you don't want to anger uncles, aunts, cousins, sisters, or brothers—especially not parents and grandparents. So, you partly obey. The very thing King Saul loved, even more than God, was his power as king, his crown. Yet, because of his disobedience, the very thing he cherished was taken from him. On that day, God rejected him as the king of Israel. At that time, no apology or act of contrition was going to change a thing. For God is not a man that He should lie, nor is He human that He will change His mind. In other words: Saul, the jig is up.

Sacrifice can be performative for all to see. But obedience is personal, because only you know what God told you to do. Saul was offering public piety to cover private rebellion. God is never impressed with optics. Man looks at the outward show, but God looks at the heart behind the action. The very same Amalekites that Saul spared showed up later, as King Agag's descendants reared their heads again as a nemesis of Israel. One act of disobedience echoed for generations.

We are to obey. We are not told to predict the waves and ripple effect; we are called to trust the One who sees the ocean.

My friends, don't let the jig be up. Remember, obedience is better than pretending your reason for not doing what God impressed upon you was for a greater purpose. You know better, and so does God. There is no better or greater purpose than doing His will.

LAW 9

CONSECRATION CANCELS COUNTERFEITS

"Wherefore, come out from among them, and be ye separate, saith the Lord, and touch not the unclean thing; and I will receive you."
—2 CORINTHIANS 6:17

Let the court of Heaven convene. Let every lying spirit take the stand. Let every diluted doctrine and dollar-store anointing be cross-examined. Because today we expose the counterfeit—and consecration is our witness.

You want divine power? You want to walk in wonder? Then the first thing God will demand is your distinction. Because divine power cannot—and will not—rest on contaminated vessels. He may use you once, but He won't dwell with divided hearts.

Power leaks where purity leaves. Anointing dries up where

attention is divided. Glory withdraws where compromise moves in.

Exhibit A? The biblical warnings against mixture. Let's enter into evidence:

- Samson: Strong enough to kill lions, but too weak to tame his lust. His strength wasn't stolen—it was surrendered on Delilah's lap. You can't sleep in sin and wake up in strength.
- Saul: Anointed, appointed, and approved. But he chose applause over obedience. He spared what God said to kill. He played politics with purity. And the oil left quietly, never to return.
- Solomon: Wisest of all men—until he loved strange women more than sacred wisdom. His affections diluted his discernment. His compromise didn't happen overnight—it happened over time.

The verdict is clear: God does not bless mixture. He does not endorse duplicity. He will not pour pure power into polluted places.

Consecration is not just moral maintenance. It is a spiritual signature—God's mark on your life that says: "This one is Mine. Set apart. Separated. Sealed."

It's not just about saying "no" to sin—it's about saying "yes" to sacredness. It's choosing the narrow when wide is easier. It's choosing silent obedience over loud opinion. It's the discipline of denial in a generation addicted to dopamine.

Greene says, "Exploit every pleasure." God says, "Crucify every idol."

Because if you refuse to kill it, it will come back to kill your calling. Whatever you won't surrender becomes your snare.

Whatever you hide becomes your hemorrhage. Whatever you justify will eventually judge you.

Don't get it twisted—this is not about legalism, it's about leverage. The devil doesn't fear your microphone—he fears your consecration. He doesn't tremble at your charisma—he trembles at your crucified life. Because demons can mimic style, but they cannot counterfeit sanctification.

- Consecration cleans the cup before God fills it.
- Consecration guards the gates before the attack comes.
- Consecration shuts the door before Delilah whispers again.

It is not your performance that preserves you—it's your purity. Not your gifting—but your gutting before God.

You don't fast just to lose weight. You fast to lose worldliness. You don't pray just to feel spiritual. You pray to kill spiritual sloth. You consecrate not because you're perfect—but because He is holy. Because His hand is on your head and His fire longs to fall—but it will not fall on flesh.

Let this be your resolution: Stay clean when culture gets corrupted. Stay hidden when everyone wants hype. Stay holy when it hurts. Stay guarded when they gossip. Stay still when it gets noisy.

Because the oil won't fall on a cluttered altar. And fire won't fill a temple built for trends. The weight of glory only rests where there's been a washing.

So, ask yourself: "Is my life sacred—or is it split? Are my words surrendered—or staged? Is my walk holy—or hybrid?"

Consecration is your covering. It keeps the counterfeit from clinging. It keeps the familiar from infecting the fire.

If you want to walk in real, residue-breaking, realm-shifting power, you must choose to be set apart—or you'll fall apart.

Don't match a world you were made to move. Don't blend with a culture you were born to break. Fast when they feast. Pray when they post. Guard your gates. Watch your walk. Be still long enough for fire to fall.

Because when Heaven searches for a soldier, it doesn't look for charisma. It looks for consecration. And when He finds it—hell trembles, and Heaven moves.

LAW 10

REVELATION PRECEDES RELEASE

"Surely the Lord God will do nothing, but he revealeth his secret unto his servants the prophets."

—AMOS 3:7

Don't step out until you have heard from Heaven. Don't start building until you've received the blueprint, for God doesn't bless a movement without giving a mandate. Revelation isn't extra, it's essential. It's not just about having direction, it's about having divine clarity. Without it, you walk in assumption. There is no power in that, and definitely no divine power. With it, you walk in authority. And to safeguard us from becoming full of ourselves, sometimes He protects us from making a complete fool of ourselves by keeping us humble. Yes, at times a stumbling block may be allowed to roll into your path, just to remind you that you are not in charge. You are simply fulfilling an assignment for a broader cause that is too wonderful for you to see it all.

Remember the apostle, Paul? He was given revelations so breathtaking and spiritually weighted that he was also given a thorn in his side (2 Corinthians 12:7). He, like many of us, couldn't see the big picture. He thought this thorn was going to hamper the mission, throw a monkey wrench in what God expected from him. Instead, this constant bother was sent to buffer him, to keep him humble, and, in fact, to make sure the mission would be completed. Once he understood the bigger picture, he thanked God for the thorn that had weakened him and concluded that when he was weak, he was then strong.

God will at times reveal things to you about you and it will resonate. He will do the same in other areas.

There is no need to waste your breath by having a conversation with the devil as many do. I see many holding hour-long conversations telling the devil to let them go, or let their child go, or how he is nothing but a liar and the father of lies. Yet we never realize that giving him time is a distraction and offers him a bit more rank and power than he deserves. If God allowed it, and continued to allow it after much prayer to Him, your time would be better spent understanding that perhaps your "thorn" was specifically placed by God to assure that you would stay on course, not veer off the track, and finish the race set before you. Have you ever thought of that? Just like the devil needed permission to touch Job, he needs permission to come after you as well. You want clarity? Go to God. He may be bringing you to a place where you find strength in your weakness, knowing that His grace is sufficient.

LAW 11

IDENTITY OVER IMAGE

"For ye are dead, and your life is hid with Christ in God."
—COLOSSIANS 3:3

In Greene's world, you recreate yourself. Be who your associates want. Morph in the moment. Wear the mask until you have won them over, then strike. But in God's kingdom, you don't manufacture identity; you receive it.

Jesus didn't "find himself" in the wilderness. He already knew who He was before the devil ever opened his mouth. You see, power does not, nor has it ever come from image. It flows from identity. And identity, at least your authentic self, is only found in the One who formed you. In the book of James, He said, "If any of you lack wisdom, let him ask of God" (1:5) and in Jeremiah, "For I know the thoughts that I think toward you, saith the Lord, thoughts of peace, and not of evil, to give you an expected end" (29:11).

You don't become powerful by pretending. You become powerful by standing still in who God says you are. Because the enemy and whoever doesn't want to see you succeed or prosper doesn't fear who you're pretending to be. In fact, they will let you continue pretending all day long, knowing that at the end of the day, you are fooling no one but yourself. But they do and will respectfully fear who you truly are, especially if they see you manifesting your God given authenticity. Once you stop pretending, stop performing, and start believing, you will be unstoppable and will discover God will do more than you can even think or imagine.

Don't chase identity: wear it, carry it, accept it. There is nothing worse than painting a Superman emblem on your chest, identifying as someone with superhuman power, and walking in that confidence only to break out into an anxious sweat when the pressure intensifies. The heat of emotional, psychological, and mental challenges can cause the painted-on identity to become distorted, start to melt away, and run down your leg, causing a puddle beneath you. That is an image that will be difficult to overcome. You can't explain it away. Your entire value system was created by a few creative colors and a big S painted on your chest, and you spent every day trying to avoid this day, but it came and went. And with its departure, you are left empty, and asking yourself, "Who am I?"

There once was a man who wore a mask. Not out of fear, but out of habit. Each day, he picked a new one from a shelf full of faces: smiling masks, strong masks, successful masks, all kinds of masks he had at his disposal. He wore them to work. He wore them to worship. He even wore them when he wept.

Behind every mask was a man who once knew his name, but now only responded to applause. He was praised for what he projected, but no one really knew him. Not even himself.

One day, the man stood before a mirror. Not a mirror of glass, but of glory. He saw himself stripped of shine, free of filters, bare as he was before the world told him who to be. And in that sacred reflection, he didn't see shame. He saw a son. Not a brand. Not a persona. Not a performer. He felt peace. He saw a beloved child, born of breath and dust, marked by mercy and made for meaning. The man wept. Not because he hated who he was, but because for the first time in a long time, he was finally able to recognize himself again.

He returned to his shelf of masks. One by one, he smashed them. Though the crowds grew quieter, the likes decreased, and the followers dropped off, his spirit grew louder. His soul sang again, but this time it sang a new song! The song it sang was of a man who chose identity over image, authenticity over applause, and truth over trend. He discovered that the world will always applaud your image as long as it entertains or benefits them, and similarly, he found out that Heaven only anoints your identity.

Let the false faces fall from you. There is no power in pretending. Only the real you can carry what God has placed in you.

LAW 12

REPENTANCE RESURRECTS POWER

"Repent ye therefore, and be converted, that your sins may be blotted out, when the times of refreshing shall come from the presence of the Lord."

—ACTS 3:19

Your God-given power doesn't leave you because of weakness. It leaves because of willful rebellion. And it returns when you repent—not perform, not pretend, but repent. David sinned quietly but repented loudly. Peter denied Jesus not once, not twice, but three times, yet repented and came back with fire.

Greene suggests: Never apologize. Never admit fault. But God says, "the sacrifices of God are a broken spirit: a broken and contrite heart, O God, thou wilt not despise" (Psalm 51:17). So, if you are feeling impotent and want to regain your edge, fall to your knees before you try to rise to the next level. Power doesn't return through spin; it comes through surrender, as repentance is the reset button of the Spirit. When sin (or that thing you know is holding you back) makes you content to tell your conscience, "nobody's perfect," knowing it's a temporary salve on a sick soul cut off—when that weight is laid aside, self-pride and willful rebellion lose their grip. Humility reconnects, and now you are one honest prayer from being resurrected back into a state of divine power. The kind that can intervene for loved ones, be strong for the weary, and provide faith lessons to the faithless. The one that says, "Follow me as I follow Christ." Not because you are better than them, but because you have tried to do it yourself and realize you were simply "smelling yourself" as they say, and couldn't recognize your own stench.

King David was a man after God's own heart. A good man, a godly man. Yet the blessings God bestowed upon him caused him to start smelling himself, assuming he was living his best life in his own power, his own strength, and his own successes. So much so that he took another man's wife as his own. He realized that was wrong, so to justify his act, he used his power and authority and leadership as king to put her husband in the first line of combat after getting him drunk to increase the risk of him becoming a casualty of war. Greene says that there is "power in resources, strategy, and control of people." Scripture says, power belongs to God (Psalm 62:11). This kind of crafty, quick-witted, deceptive, manipulative, and self-serving display of power may be found in other books about power, but the result that is not discussed is self-destruction.

David's plans were successful. He now had his woman. They had a child...but the child became sick and died. God visited David and told him he had had the Lord's favor and could have had anything he wanted, but in his selfishness he took another man's wife. He told David that because of those treacherous acts, he would have trouble in his own household. Notice that

I did not say God would make or cause trouble to come into his household, but with divine foresight, He saw it coming. In another place, He said the sins of the father will visit the children, grandchildren, and great-grandchildren for the sins of those who hate Him, to the third and fourth generation. That is to say that your father's behaviors—your lifestyle, your "secret sins" that were not so secret—have permeated your household and are now mimicked and duplicated, often with more voracity than the generation before, for three to four generations until someone breaks the curse and stops the cycle. This is why King David's self-serving behaviors were passed down to his sons. Amnon, his son, desired his stepsister, so he raped her. Absalom wanted David's throne, so he stole the hearts of the people through seductive power. He used his height, his good looks, and his thick wavy hair to woo the crowds, and in the end, it was his thick wavy hair that snared him to his death in tree branches while he was trying to escape enemies.

And if that wasn't enough bad luck, David, who was still king, had to get up and go to work. While doing battle, he was victorious and had the audacity to tell one of his military leaders to count the troops. The commander tried to tell the king that pride and self-reliance were at the core of this request. David wouldn't listen, and his pompous attitude brought punishment to Israel. The Bible says the devil rose up amongst the troops. The spirit of Satan was amongst them and tempted David to look and see all he had done in his own strength, and it cost him and the whole nation.

Sin, while often appealing, will always take you further than you intended to go, keep you longer than you intended to stay, and will cost you more than you intended to pay. Remember that.

His humanness lured him to try a Greene-like power trip and it cost him dearly. Seventy thousand men of Israel died from the plague, so his personal self-serving pride had corporate consequences. His self-consumed mind took many lives. Like many of us know, everything that sounds good ain't good. It's not how greatly you do it but how long you can do it greatly. Resting in a power of manipulation and exploiting others' weaknesses will eventually come back to you. Your chickens will come home to roost, and the eggs they hatch will magnify the effect of the seeds you planted. You will reap the harvest you have sown, be it good or bad—and there is nothing good about exploiting others, deceiving others, manipulating people, capitalizing on their vulnerabilities, etc. No matter how you try to justify it as "human nature."

David was tired of this game, and in Psalm 51:1 (KJV) we find out how he broke the horrible rut he found himself in by chasing power and he shares his repentance with us. He writes, "Have mercy upon me, O God, according to thy lovingkindness: according unto the multitude of thy tender mercies blot out my transgressions…" He goes on to say in verse 12, "Restore unto me the joy of thy salvation; and uphold me with thy free spirit."

His soul was sick and like your body rejecting bad meat with violent vomiting, he was vomiting out all the things he thought was good and hearty for him but was killing his discernment, spiritual maturity, and divine connection. David was restored. He realized, to get power and peace to return to his life, it wasn't about staying on the same path and just trying to do things a little differently. He had to totally reject that highway. He'd been on it long enough to know it was a road that, when he finally got to where he thought he wanted to be, he would look up and find himself completely lost and out of the presence of God. So, he got off that road, turned around and went in another direction. Anything other than an about face isn't repentance and will end up being more of the same.

This is a good time to pause and reflect. Before we go any further, I want to ask: have you made some of the same mistakes as David? All of his missteps had pride at their core. His crown gave him the big head, his clout robbed him of empathy and sensitivity to others' needs. He became a self-serving leader and occasionally had to flex to brag about his own military strength, and credit as commander-in-chief. Maybe you are not a king, but you might be the head of your household, or a team leader at work, or in your chosen sport. How are you using the power given to you? And how are you trying to obtain said power? On the backs of others while taking all the credit? Yeah, as mere mortals, these thoughts are not too far from our thinking, but we can bring every thought captive to the obedience of God's Word. And the first step is to repent of the thought, before it becomes an act. We have the power of choice. Choose not to stifle the divine power flowing within you by making an about face from thoughts and urges that we all have from time to time and must deal with. Thoughts that can lead to our detriment of power, the kind that comes from above.

LAW 13

THE SECRET PLACE SECURES PUBLIC POWER

"But thou, when thou prayest, enter into thy closet, and when thou hast shut thy door, pray to thy Father which is in secret; and thy Father...shall reward thee openly."

—MATTHEW 6:6

You can't carry divine power publicly if you're empty privately. Jesus withdrew often—not because He was weak, but because He was wise. Before He fed crowds, He fed on being in the presence of God. Before He healed others, He was hidden with His Father, fortifying His wholeness.

Greene says: stay visible, stay dominant. God says: "He that dwelleth in the secret place of the most High shall abide under the shadow of the Almighty" (Psalm 91:1). So, my friend, your source isn't the crowd, it's the closet. No secret place equals no sustained divine power; to know a secret place means coming to know divine power in your life. Your power gets diminished from not making time to refuel. It's not lack of skill that depletes you but lack of stillness. Having power without being in His presence is performance. Be sure to get back to that place of solitude with God where no one sees you, so that you are ready when everyone sees you.

"Let us therefore come boldly unto the throne of grace, that we may obtain mercy, and find grace to help in time of need." This is a popular verse found in Hebrews 4:16, but what does it mean, and how does it apply to divine power? Well, I am glad you asked, because I don't want you to mistake silence for stagnation, or solitude for weakness. I don't want you to overlook the secret place.

This verse tells us how to come: boldly! Not timid, not trembling like beggars at the back door. No. Come as blood-bought children. Come as image-bearers of divine design. Come as those who know the veil has been torn and the invitation is still warm from Heaven's breath.

This verse tells us where to come: to the throne of grace. Not a throne of performance. Not a seat of shame, but a throne dripping with mercy, saturated in sympathy, and sovereign in strength. A throne that doesn't condemn the weary, but crowns them!

It tells us why to come: to find grace and mercy. Mercy for sin behind you. Grace for the assignment ahead of you. It is not a throne of judgement. It's a fountain of a just-enough, right-on-time kind of power.

It tells us when to come: in our time of need. Which means, right now. Not when you are ready. Not when you've performed, but when you are in need, empty, drained, and dry.

That is the power of the secret place. It's where the real ones go when the fake ones post. It's where the fire falls for those who dare to kneel before they command.

Elijah didn't use his power on Mount Carmel. He prayed for it in private. He bowed low before fire came from on high. He got quiet before Heaven got loud. And when the prophets of Baal danced and shouted, Elijah whispered, and God answered with flame.

You see, dear friend, Heaven still backs the bowed. And God still honors the hidden. The secret place is not a suggestion, it's a summons. Not a spare room in your spiritual house; it's the inner room, the upper room, and the holy of holies. It's the power plant from which everything else draws its current. So, if you want public power, then you must walk through private portals. This is not about performance. It's about presence.

So, go! Go to your closet, your car, your kitchen floor. Go where nobody but God sees. And seek Him, weep if you must, go to war against the forces against you via private worship. For when you kneel in private, He moves in public on your behalf.

He still rewards the ones who come in secret. He still exalts the ones who bow before they battle. And He still responds with mercy, with grace, and sometimes…with fire from on high.

LAW 14

GRATITUDE GATHERS GRACE

"In every thing give thanks: for this is the will of God in Christ Jesus concerning you."

—1 THESSALONIANS 5:18

Before Jesus broke the bread and fed the multitude, He lifted it up and gave thanks. He didn't wait for more. He blessed what was already in His hands.

Gratitude is not just a gesture, it's a gateway. It opens access to grace, and it is through this access that divine power flows freely. Not because you earned it, but because you honored it.

Jesus had just fed five thousand men, not counting women and children. A miraculous feast from a boy's lunch. But let's look again. This wasn't just a story of God's provision. It was also a test of posture.

Some followed Jesus only for the loaves. They wanted the product, not the presence. They wanted a miracle without a message, a meal without a master. And when Jesus began to shift from feeding flesh to feeding faith, they got full, and then they got gone. "...You seek me, not because you saw the signs, but because you ate of the loaves and were filled" (John 6:26 NKJV).

They were consumers of quick gratification, not carriers of lasting gratitude. They only saw Jesus as a means to satisfy their appetite, not as the end of their searching. When He offered eternal life instead of an extra piece of fish, they walked away. "From that time, many of his disciples turned back and walked with him no more" (John 6:66 NKJV).

But then there were the few.

The ones who didn't leave. The ones who saw the miracle and stayed for the messenger. They didn't just want full bellies, they wanted full hearts. They knew any other path would be a downgrade. No other voice spoke to their soul. No other door held the keys. Peter said, "Lord, to whom shall we go? thou hast the words of eternal life" (John 6:68). Let me say it again: no human voice—not Greene, or any other voice of the broad way—has the final say on the power word for yesterday, today, or tomorrow. But Jesus has words eternal!

Peter's proclamation is gratitude talking, grace receiving, and divine power in the making.

Gratitude isn't about what's in your hand. It's about who holds your heart. The crowd was after what they could grab. The faithful were after who they could grow under. Gratitude is the soil where grace takes root. It says, "Even if the meal ends, I'm still staying, because YOU are the source."

Understand this: God doesn't pour power into entitlement. He pours it into those who come back to say thanks.

So here comes the purifying fire.

Do you only worship when you're full? Or do you still follow when the manna ends, and dinner is over, when the miracle becomes a message that demands more than flesh, that asks for faith?

Divine power flows best through grateful vessels. Not entitled. Not envious. But deeply thankful, even when it's not enough yet.

Greene teaches gain. But gratitude? That's Heaven's economics. It opens doors that money can not. It draws grace to your feet like manna in the morning.

Gratitude is power's invitation. It positions your heart for provision that doesn't spoil, for favor that doesn't fade, and for grace that multiplies even when the crowd is gone and the followers are few. Gratitude doesn't just receive bread. It stays for the baker. And in staying, it unlocks the flow of grace that empowers you to act publicly because you have honored Him privately.

LAW 15

INTIMACY WITH GOD IS THE HIGHEST INFLUENCE

"Draw nigh to God, and he will draw nigh to you..."
—JAMES 4:8

Moses said, "...if thy presence go not with me, carry us not up hence" (Exodus 33:15).

Now that's a man who understood influence begins with intimacy. Greene obsesses over influence, how to craft perception, and control behaviors. But the Bible states that favor flows from friendship with God, just as friendship with the world and its views means enmity (hatred) against God (James 4:4).

Abraham was considered a friend of God. John laid his head on Jesus's chest. These men moved nations, not through networking but in knowing God. Influence that doesn't come from intimacy is empty.

People we can fool, but you can't fake a friendship with God. Power isn't in your pitch, it's in your proximity to the throne.

Biblically speaking, a person with a friendship, or in intimate fellowship with God, is often referred to as one who walks with God. Like best friends who can take a stroll in the park and talk for days, having no secrets yet knowing each other's most shameful and regretful moments. It's a relationship where vulnerability isn't a weakness but becomes a strength. So it is with God; to walk with him is not casual, it's covenantal. It is not a pace, it is proximity. It is not a religious routine but a relational rhythm with the divine.

In Scripture this phrase isn't tossed around loosely. Only a few bore this distinction. And their stories didn't just echo obedience, they radiated Heaven's approval.

The first was Enoch: the man who disappeared into glory. "And Enoch walked with God: and he was not; for God took him" (Genesis 5:24). Enoch's life wasn't defined by miracles or military might. It was marked by moment-by-moment intimacy. He didn't lead a nation. He didn't part a sea. He simply walked closely with God, and that walk translated him to glory.

The second was Noah: the man who built what had never been seen. "…Noah was a just man and perfect in his generations, and Noah walked with God" (Genesis 6:9). When the world was wicked, Noah didn't blend in; he played it forward. He didn't need confirmation; he had a conversation with God. He walked with God, and that walk gave him warnings others couldn't hear, and wisdom to build what the world mocked until it was too late. He had foresight in a foolish world. While others party in ignorant bliss, those who walk with God are always prepared for what's coming. In his divine power, he saved not only himself but also his family.

That same insight and divine power is available to you, too.

He is the same God of yesterday, today, and forevermore. Times change, views change, the world changes…but God is the constant whose insights, truths, and governance to those who walk with Him are not limited by time, place, or space. He is forever present. Commit yourself to a daily walk with Him, and before long, you won't have to talk to convince anyone of your power that is worthy to be respected; your walk will talk for you in a way that can not be denied or overlooked.

LAW 16

FAITH FRAMES YOUR FUTURE

"Now faith is the substance of things hoped for, the evidence of things not seen."

—HEBREWS 11:1

Faith is more than a belief, it's spiritual blueprinting. It builds what eyes haven't seen. It draws power to weak places. It calls down things not yet and makes them now. Through faith, you don't stumble into your destiny, you speak it until it stands. You believe it until it breathes.

Friend, listen to me. Your future listens to the tone of your faith. Don't speak small and expect spiritual power. Say it! Believe it! Build it!

Faith is not fantasy, it's a framework. It is the steel structure behind what has yet to manifest. Faith is substance, not emotion, not energy, not empty positivity. It is proof of what will be, even when there is no sign of it yet.

Faith is foundational. Not just to Christianity but to divine power itself. Faith is the foundation of function, "Through faith…the worlds were framed…" (Hebrews 11:3 NKJV), and since God framed the universe with His words, then your words must align with your belief if you want to see divine power flow because "…without faith it is impossible to please him…"(Hebrews 11:6 NIV). There is no substitute for it. Not sacrifice, not service, not spiritual performance. You don't attract and get Heaven's attention by your hustle, you align by believing Him boldly.

The heroes of Hebrews 11 weren't dreamers—they were doers.

- By faith, Noah built.
- By faith, Abraham obeyed.
- By faith, Moses chose.
- By faith, Rahab welcomed.

Faith didn't make them passive. It made them powerful. And real faith has a footprint, so you can track it. You can see its sweat and scars. It isn't silent, it speaks through strategy, sacrifice, stamina, and service.

Faith is the language of the future spoken in a present that doesn't yet comprehend or agree. It sees destiny in the deserts, rain in the droughts, and resurrection in the graves. It calls what is not as though it already is, and then builds like it's already done (Romans 4:17). That's faith! It's also divine power! And it is the foundation of everything else in this book.

You can have anointing. You can have alignment with the things of God. You can even have an assignment. But if you don't have faith, you won't move mountains, you will just be in awe of them and feel like the job you've been given is insurmountable. Relying only on your human effort will often cause you to be overcome by the waves and sink instead of keeping your eyes on the One who empowered you to walk on water. Life will often challenge our faith and temporarily cause us to focus on the mountain and the waves, instead of forging through to move the mountain and walk on the water to the other side.

So, in a world that likes to flex and even crush others with their power, you are different, you are built different. If you flex, flex your faith. Step up and step out. Frame it in faith, not fear. Frame it with vision, not vibes. Call it before it comes. Walk it before it's seen. Build the boat, though the skies are clear. Speak rain in the drought, whisper life in the tomb of a dying relationship and bring it back to life. Dig trenches in the valley before a single cloud blooms.

Faith is not a fantasy. It's the framework of your future. It's Heaven's construction code and doubt is the demolition crew sent to steal your blueprint. Don't let your eyes rob your spirit. Don't let the "not yet" silence the "He said." Frame it in faith: speak it before it stands, sow when it looks like famine, stretch when it feels like failing. Believe in the dark what He showed in the light and build like you never saw the night. Because faith…it's the bridge between what was spoken and what will stand. It's not always loud, but it's never late. It doesn't flinch when feelings change. It doesn't fold when others flee.

Frame it. Fuel it. Fight for it. Your future is already fortified if you have the faith to just follow through.

LAW 17

REJECTION IS DIVINE REDIRECTION

"'I know thy works: behold, I have set before thee an open door, and no man can shut it...'"

—REVELATION 3:8

Consider this for those moments when it seems like your plans didn't work out: they didn't call you back for that job you claimed and prayed for. They didn't invite you for an interview. They laughed at the vision. Your partner dumped you without any forewarning or clues. Well...perfect!

In God's realm, rejection isn't random, it's redirection. Granted, this is not a divine power that we see readily. It is one that can be seen through the eyes of faith, as well as during our time of reflection and understanding of God's commitment to our greatness. Humanly speaking, rejection often hits differently. It can potentially make us question ourselves, or worse...the God who has brought us this far. Just understand there are forces at work at all times. Forces to bring us down, forces to lift us up. Forces that want us to forsake God, and those that want us to lean into our faith more through the rough patches.

Joseph was destined for leadership and greatness. However, looking at his life early on, it looked to be the opposite. Just remember, in a good book, some chapters may sadden you, others may bore you, and some…well, they can have you so motivated and thinking you can do anything! What makes you not give up and close the book when it gets sad often depends on your knowledge of the author. The Bible declares that "Being confident of this very thing, that he which hath begun a good work in you will perform it until the day of Jesus Christ" (Philippians 1:6), and "…we know that all things work together for good to them that love God, to them who are the called according to his purpose" (Romans 8:28), and "Looking unto Jesus the author and finisher of our faith…" (Hebrews 12:2). So then, with the rejection, trust that it's the end of that chapter, and it's time to turn the page to the next, trusting that it will end well.

Joseph's story makes it clearer how God moves at times. He had God's favor and his father's, too, for that matter. He was rejected by his own siblings, but little did they know, though they meant it for evil, God meant it for good. Their shutting the door on Joseph was God's sovereignty at work, using life's events to carry out His perfect will in his life. Joseph went from being Potiphar's slave to Pharaoh's seer by interpreting Pharaoh's dream and saving an entire country from starvation—including his own brothers who rejected him.

This is one of those attributes of manifesting divine power that will take some acceptance. Because we are cloaked in flesh, it will sting if and when you are rejected, but if you can maintain this divine perspective, you will continue to trust God through the process and cause others to marvel at your resilience and strength during a time when most would be devastated and overcome with self-doubt. You, too, may have had these feelings. But now, understanding the big picture, you can have a different perspective as you watch with grace and gratitude at the wonderful things God is about to do in your life.

LAW 18

THE WORD IS YOUR WEAPON

"For the word of God is quick, and powerful, and sharper than any twoedged sword..."

—HEBREWS 4:12

Jesus didn't fight Satan and his influences with charisma, He fought him with Scripture. Power in Greene's book depends on cleverness and cunning. Divine power rests on what God has already said. You don't need to fabricate new words, just remember.

You cannot walk in divine power without wielding the divine Word of God. You may wear the armor. You may even fast and pray. But without the Word, you are dressed for battle with nothing to strike with. Because of all the armor God gives us, only one is offensive—the sword of the Spirit, which is the Word of God.

We don't fight with fists. We fight with phrases spoken by

Heaven. We don't conquer with charisma. We conquer with covenant language. And yet, many have mishandled the Word. Misquoted it. Misunderstood it. Misused it. And then wondered why their mountains didn't move. Why their prayers hit ceilings. Why their fire faded in the furnace.

You asked and received it not because you asked amiss (James 4:3). You wield a sword, but it's dull from lack of study, bent by bad doctrine, and rusty from disuse.

Even prayer itself must be Word-anchored. Without the Word, your passion becomes presumption. "So then faith comes by hearing, and hearing by the word of God" (Romans 10:17 NKJV).

You want faith that moves mountains? Then you need the Word that moves Heaven.

The Word is not to be used like a buffet. You don't get to pick and choose what blesses you and bypass what breaks you. You must read it contextually, prayerfully, and obediently.

Isaiah describes the process best: "...precept upon precept, line upon line..." (Isaiah 28:10 ESV).

You can not live by isolated verses and expect integrated victories. The Word must be eaten whole to work holy. Immature hearts choke on strong truth. They want prophecy without principle. They want power without process. But the Word of righteousness is for the spiritually mature, who by constant use have trained themselves to discern between good and evil (Hebrews 5:13–14).

Jesus gave us this parable, but life reveals the patterns.

1. The Dull Listener: Heard the Word, but didn't value it. The devil snatched it away like a crow from the pavement. No reverence. No retention. No result.
2. The Deceived Listener: Heard the Word, got excited,

shouted at church, said "amen"—but never rooted. So, when life scorched their soul, their shallow soil couldn't hold the seed, and they fell away. Emotion is not endurance.
3. The Distracted Listener: Heard the Word, but loved the world. Choked by the thorns of busyness, bitterness, and broken priorities. The word became one of many voices influencing them and thus produced no power.
4. The Devoted Listener: Heard the Word, received it, kept it, and bore fruit. Thirtyfold. Sixtyfold. One hundred times over. Because they didn't just get the seed, they stewarded the soil.

When Satan tempted Jesus, Jesus didn't shout. He spoke the Word. "It is written…" (Matthew 4:1–11). Three times He swung the sword, and hell had no counter. Why? Because Jesus didn't just quote it, He embodied it.

Yes, faith is foundational, but faith comes by hearing, and power comes by doing. Don't just hear the Word, heed it. Don't just quote Scripture, become Scripture in motion. Let the Word dwell richly, but precisely, and lead divinely. Because when you master the Word, you won't just win arguments—you win battles.

You will pray with precision. Prophesy with purpose. And stand when others fall, not because you're stronger…but because you're standing on the rock of the written Word.

It is the chief cornerstone from which your entire being must be built. Then and only then will you have what it takes to withstand whatever comes your way and become more than a conqueror. Not only that, it's the divine power that can be sown into another that God's will may be done in their life as well. Now that is power!

PART I SUMMARY

You've just walked through the first eighteen laws—pillars, postures, and principles that don't fracture. These laws were not lofty theories but soul-deep truths, chiseling your character into a vessel fit for Heaven's voltage.

You discovered that weakness is not your wall, but your womb. That humility is not humiliation, but Heaven's headquarters. That silence is not absence, but a sacred strategy. You've learned that waiting is not wasting, but weaponry in disguise.

Through brokenness, you found boldness. Through obedience, you discovered outcomes were secondary to intimacy. You learned that consecration channels away counterfeits, and that revelation always precedes release. You've been reminded that identity outweighs image, and that repentance resurrects power.

In the secret place you secured public power, in gratitude you gathered grace, and in intimacy you touched true influence. Faith reframed your future, and rejection redirected your steps toward divine redirection. By the time you lifted up the Word as your weapon, the foundation beneath your feet had shifted—no longer sand, but stone.

This part—Foundation—was never about show, it was about soil. Every chapter tilled your ground, pulled up weeds of pride and pretense, and planted the seed of surrender. Every law anchored you, not in platforms, but in purpose; not in resumes, but in readiness.

You are no longer tossed by the applause of men—you are tethered to the approval of God. And now, as you step from foundation to function, remember: what has been buried has not been lost. It has been planted. What felt like breaking was actually building. And what seemed like silence was God setting the stage.

You've been grounded. Rooted. Reset. And now, God can grow what you've submitted.

So, take a breath. Wipe the dirt from your hands. You've been built deep. Now we move from foundation to function—where the planted become the powerful, and the formed begin to flow.

PART II

THE FUNCTION OF DIVINE POWER

Greene's laws function through tactical deception, control of perception, and social manipulation. For example: his third law says conceal your intentions, his sixth says court attention at all costs, and his fifteenth commands you to crush your enemy totally. All of which are stitched together to preserve power through psychological warfare, treating people as pawns and problems rather than neighbors and souls.

But where Greene's power functions through secrecy, seduction, and suppression, divine power functions through clarity, calling, and character. We are not called to conceal but to confess, not to deceive but to declare. The function of divine power is servanthood, not stagecraft; it is truth-telling, not theatrics.

This is where theory becomes testimony. Function is faith in motion. It's how you treat your coworker who just gossiped about you, how you speak truth in a meeting where lies are easier, how you choose generosity when greed is applauded. Divine function doesn't hide behind smoke and mirrors, but it shows up in the small spaces: making eye contact with the overlooked, answering the phone when your teenager is in crisis, resisting the urge to clap back with venom when someone slanders your name.

Greene hands you a tool belt filled with masks, mirrors, and manipulation. But when the storm settles, nothing of substance remains. Divine power, on the other hand, equips you with tools that build what lasts: integrity over intrigue, compassion over camouflage, clarity over cunning.

Here's the shift: don't just admire divine power, apply it. Function means asking yourself in the moment, "Am I choosing character or charisma? Calling or clout? Service or spotlight?" Because when function flows from the flesh, the mission malfunctions. But when function flows from the Father, fruit multiplies—in your home, your workplace, your ministry, your daily walk.

So, step across this bridge with me. Foundation has been laid. Now function must be lived.

LAW 19

SERVING UNLOCKS SUPERNATURAL STRATEGY

"But he that is greatest among you shall be your servant."
—MATTHEW 23:11

Power flexes. Real power bows. Worldly power demands a pedestal. Divine power kneels at the feet of the forgotten.

Jesus didn't wash feet because He lacked status. He washed them because He owned it. And He still stooped. Still served. Still scrubbed the dust off the very feet that would walk away when He needed them most.

Let that sink in.

In a world where everyone wants their name in lights, divine power says: "If you want to rise, start low. If you want authority, start with a towel." Greene teaches: make them serve you. Jesus teaches: if you're too big to serve, you're too small to lead.

From Genesis to Revelation, the strategy of Heaven has always included the scandal of servanthood.

- Joseph served in Pharaoh's prison before he stood in Pharaoh's palace.
- Ruth served Naomi before she entered Boaz's field.
- David served Saul with songs before he ever picked up a scepter.
- Jesus served bread at the table of betrayal—and still gave Judas a seat.

Why? Because in God's economy, service is not a sidebar—it's the blueprint. It doesn't delay destiny. It develops it. Serving isn't a detour from power. It is the door to it.

Jesus could have called angels to carry His cross—but He carried it Himself. He could have silenced the soldiers—but He washed His disciples instead. Because true power doesn't parade. It pours. It pours oil. It pours time. It pours tears. It pours identity into others until their crushed shells become vessels of glory too.

Greene says: manipulate the moment. God says: minister in the margins.

Greene says: appear untouchable. Jesus says: touch the untouchables.

Greene says: demand loyalty. Heaven says: demonstrate love. And love that doesn't serve isn't love at all.

Let's fast-forward to a man who walked this law out loud—Tim Tebow. Football icon? Yes. Heisman winner? Indeed. But his greatest plays never made ESPN. They happened in orphanages. In hospital rooms. In congressional hearings for trafficked children. While others chased brands, he chased brokenness. While some flexed endorsements, he poured his platform into empowering the least of these.

This wasn't charity. This was supernatural strategy. He tethered his identity to purpose. He sacrificed spotlight to shine it on others. And in doing so, he showed us that real power is always undercover before it's undeniable.

No marketing team needed. No viral post required. Just a man on mission, moving quietly, but shaking eternity.

"If I then, your Lord and Master, have washed your feet; ye also ought to wash one another's feet."

—JOHN 13:14

Why did Jesus serve? Not for applause, but to inaugurate a Kingdom culture where the towel is greater than the title. He knew something we must never forget: Serving doesn't shrink your significance. It sanctifies it. It doesn't demote your destiny. It develops it. It doesn't dilute your power. It directs it.

Serving is sacred warfare. It breaks cycles of self-obsession. It builds platforms of purpose. It's how you confuse demons and confound kings—by going low when the world says go loud.

Make no mistake—serving is not weakness. It is war. It's how Moses won battles with arms lifted in intercession. It's how Stephen saw Heaven open as he was being stoned, because he served even his killers with forgiveness. It's how Jesus defeated death—not by descending in fire, but by hanging in surrender.

You want to win spiritual battles? Pick up a basin. Grab a towel. Feed the hungry. Answer the call. Hold the door. Mentor the youth. Visit the prisoner. Be kind to your Judas.

Because when you serve without a spotlight, you tap into a strategy hell can't track. And Heaven cannot help but respond.

So, if you're called to lead, then you're first called to serve. Pick up the towel—not to clean up messes but to reveal miracles. Don't wait for a platform—find a person in need. Don't seek to be elevated—lean down until divine power flows through you like a river.

For in the end, the highest King stooped the lowest. And the cross wasn't the defeat of divine power—it was its greatest demonstration.

Let them chase crowns. You? Chase the call. And when they ask how you got so far, so fast, with so little—tell them: "I just kept serving."

LAW 20

DISCERNMENT GUIDES DOMINION

"Prove all things; hold fast that which is good."
—1 THESSALONIANS 5:21

Samson had strength, but no discernment to be able to peel back Delilah's motives. Solomon had wisdom, and with it he preserved the throne. It is a needed power in a world seeking to always get the upper hand. More importantly, when used maximally, it is to build and edify, to find the truth in a situation by making assessments of actions in deed and words that often reveal motive and the true intents of the heart. This comes naturally—or shall I say supernaturally—to the man or woman empowered by God.

However, there has been much said about other terms like intuition, instinct, and emotional intelligence, which can closely align with spiritual discernment. This overlap can also mislead as to what discernment as a divine power actually is.

Spiritual discernment is the gift of the Spirit. Often hailed as a supernatural gift (1 Corinthians 12), spiritual discernment is God's eyes within us. It perceives spiritual realities—divine, human, and demonic, even when invisible. It alerts us to false spirits or deceptive prophecy. Acts 16 exalts believers who "discerned" the spirits behind a slave girl. It is not merely intuition, it is revelation, born of intimacy with the Spirit (Hebrews 5:14) and a foundational tool for purity, safety, and kingdom strategy. It comes by Spirit-taught words (1 Corinthians 2:13). It guards the church from spiritual terrorism: false teaching, demonic interference, and counterfeit signs. It's a gift but also a responsibility as all believers are called to test words and spirits.

Emotional discernment is often misunderstood as mere instinct, but modern psychology defines emotional intelligence (EQ or emotional quotient) with precision: EQ is the skill of perceiving, understanding, managing, and using emotions, whether our own or those of others. High EQ anchors us in reality. It recognizes underlying emotional patterns, filters, and biases, and alerts us to interpersonal pitfalls. Without emotional acuity, we are susceptible to projecting wounds or misreading motives. EQ can be strengthened through self-reflection, therapy, spiritual guidance, and intentional learning. It's not a substitute for spiritual insight, but a steward of it as it helps you apply spiritual guidance wisely in the flesh.

Discernment is also a cultivated skill, born of knowledge, history, and disciplined reflection.

It's the ability to notice objective differences and make nuanced judgements among stimuli, people, and scenarios. Growing your discernment is a lifelong process; it's never static. True discernment goes beyond intuition: it uses information, contextual understanding, and sound reasoning. It requires humility to recognize blind spots, acknowledge limits, and stay teachable. It combines head and heart, clarity of intellect and purity of spirit.

You may recall Solomon's story and how he was so wise that he wrote the Book of Proverbs. It was in the city of Gibeon, in the quiet hours of the night, when young King Solomon was confronted by the Ancient of Days. Yes, God Himself appeared in a dream and laid before Solomon a blank check of Heaven's treasury: "Ask what I shall give you" (1 Kings 3:5).

> Pause here—what would most men choose?
>
> Riches? Revenge? Long life?
>
> Wouldn't the crown already tilted on his head have whispered for more power, more prestige, more permanence?
>
> But Solomon, son of David, son of promise, opened his mouth and poured out a prayer that was not greedy, but needy.
>
> He confessed his youth, his inexperience, his insufficiency.
>
> He did not clamor for castles or clout, but for clarity of judgment.
>
> He asked for a discerning heart—
>
> a mind sharp enough to separate truth from trickery,
>
> a spirit sensitive enough to distinguish right from wrong,
>
> a wisdom wide enough to govern God's great people.
>
> And Heaven leaned in.
>
> Scripture says the saying pleased the Lord.
>
> God was moved, not by the might of Solomon's request, but by the meekness of it.
>
> Because he did not ask for his enemies' demise,
>
> because he did not ask for wealth or longevity,
>
> but for discernment to administer justice—

> God granted him what no king before or after could claim:
>
> wisdom like the waves, insight like the sunrise, understanding unmatched in all the earth.
>
> But here's the rhythm of divine reciprocity:
>
> When you seek first discernment, dominion follows.
>
> When you prioritize judgment, God provides jewels.
>
> When you crave wisdom, wealth and honor come chasing after you.
>
> So, the Lord not only crowned Solomon with wisdom beyond measure,
>
> He poured out riches and honor until his name echoed in every nation.
>
> Discernment guided his dominion, and dominion was girded by divine favor.

When all three dimensions align—spiritual insight, emotional wisdom, and acquired skill—you are no longer guessing, you're governed by godly wisdom:

- Spiritual discernment gives clarity from Heaven.
- Emotional intelligence mediates responses with grace and wisdom.
- Acquired skill ensures informed, wise decisions are grounded in reality.

It is this synergy in how this law becomes a function for your daily power-packed life. Remember, you can't rule what you can't first recognize, and a lot of what we see first is a person's emotional response as well as our own.

However, we must take care not to misuse discernment or allow the different types of knowledge to become misaligned.

Emotional savvy without spiritual alignment can lead to manipulation or paranoia. Spiritual gifts without EQ can lead to harshness or misinterpretation. Knowledge without humility can turn discernment into cognitive pride.

So let's safeguard ourselves from imploding on our own blessings by applying a practical discernment checklist to keep us from self-destruction.

1. Pray first. Ask the Spirit for guidance.
2. Check your emotions. Are you reacting or responding?
3. Gather context. Consider history, motives, and outcomes.
4. Test it. Is it aligned with Scripture? Does it lead to peace and fruit?
5. Act. Move with courage, clarity, and compassion.

Divine dominion isn't granted to the loud. It's given to those who discern. Those who hear beyond the obvious, respond beyond their feelings, and move beyond their understanding in alignment with Heaven's heart. Now that's discernment. Not guesswork, not intuition, but intelligent insight supernaturally empowered and spiritually transformative.

LAW 21

PEACE IS THE PROOF OF POWER

"Thou wilt keep him in perfect peace, whose mind is stayed on thee: because he trusteth in thee."

—ISAIAH 26:3

Jesus slept through a storm. That is power. Not noise. Not bravado, but peace.

Greene tells you to stir the waters, stay in control. God tells you to carry peace like a weapon. Power doesn't need panic to prove it's real. Divine power stills storms, starting with the one inside of you.

Learn that if they can rattle you, they can redirect you—and if they redirected you, then you are no longer in control, but being controlled. True power is poised. It's still. It is unshakeable.

In the pictorial language of Scripture, the psalmist said, "Thou preparest a table before me in the presence of mine enemies…" (Psalm 23:5). Now that's peace. To be able to sit down, fold the napkin over your lap, bow, and thank God for the food you are about to receive with no appetite lost, no stomach in knots, and knowing full well that haters run amok around you. You know you're surrounded by those lying to you, looking to sabotage your world, looking to cause trouble, scheming to get you out of your zone, and yet you slice into your steak, take a bite, and crunch on a piece of just-right asparagus and savor the flavors, giving no thought or care to the lies being told. Now that's divine power manifesting as peace!

Real power doesn't panic. It rests. Real strength doesn't shout. It settles. Because when you are in God's will, your soul becomes steel, and your mind becomes still, and your steps stay sealed, even in the storm.

In Daniel 3, we see that Shadrach, Meshach, and Abednego didn't draw swords when commanded to bow down to the Babylonian king or be thrown into a fiery furnace. They didn't scream. They didn't sweat. They stood. Calm, collected, and confident in the covenant of their God, the way-maker, who always makes a way out of no way. They said, "Oh king, we will not bow. Our God is able to deliver us. But even if he doesn't… we still won't bend." That is the kind of peace I am talking about. That kind of peace is powerful. That is the fire not just around them, but the fire within them, a fire hotter than the furnace, yet never consuming their composure. Yes, they may have had heat all around them, but they had ice in their veins as they remained cool under pressure.

Before he was a name in textbooks, Mohandas K. Gandhi was a frail-framed man with a fiery faith, who led India's struggle for independence not with swords or spears, but with silence, fasting, and nonviolent resistance. He taught the world that peace could be sharper than a blade, stronger than an army, and swifter than vengeance. Gandhi once declared: "Each one has to find his peace from within. And peace to be real must be unaffected by outside circumstances."

And across another continent, Nelson Mandela bore the bars of a prison cell for twenty-seven long years, his body bound but his spirit unbroken. When he walked free, he chose forgiveness over fury, reconciliation over revenge. To him, peace was not simply quiet skies—it was justice, freedom, and dignity for all. Mandela reminded us: "Peace is not merely the absence of war."

This is a supernatural kind of peace. A divine, powerful peace.

Daniel faced threats of being thrown into the lion's den if he didn't comply with King Darius' decree that no one should pray or petition any God for thirty days; they could only petition the king. But Daniel kept praying anyway to his God. He didn't beg for mercy when that decree came down. He didn't run and hide. He didn't hustle up a legal team. He opened the window, looked toward the East, and prayed as he always did. It was business as usual as if the lions were like lullabies, like peace was oxygen that he breathed in every second. It was as if he were already free, even before the angel showed up and shut the lion's mouth. He was in the center of God's will.

That's the only time this divine power is manifested to this degree: when you have surrendered to God's purpose and plan for your life.

And what about Stephen, the man who was stoned for his sermon? While beaten down, he looked up, face shining like an angel. Not because the rocks didn't hurt, but because the peace preceded the pain, and its power outlasted the persecution.

True peace isn't the absence of problems. It is the presence of purpose. It is the table prepared in the middle of madness. It's sipping still waters while shadows stalk. It's sleeping in the storm like Jesus in the boat while the disciples screamed and got ready to bail. Peace isn't passive, it's potent. It is proof that you are postured in promise. You can't conjure this kind of peace. You can't counterfeit it with cash. You can't manufacture it with mantras. If it flows from the Father and it floods those who walk in their divine assignment.

It doesn't matter the assignment or circumstance. Whether it's:

- a father raising sons in a wicked generation;
- a mother raising daughters in a world that promotes female lewdness and brash behavior;
- a teacher teaching in a toxic school;
- a CEO surrounded by a slither of snakes; or
- a saint praying through his pit of depression

…when you know who you are, whose you are, and why you are alive—peace is your proof.

So let the nation rage, let the furnace roar, let the lions circle, let the Judas in your life get in close because if you are in His will, then you are in His wind. And He will cause you to soar in spite of it all as there is no storm that can sink you. He will keep in perfect peace the one whose mind is stayed on Him.

That is divine power. That's the flex of Heaven. That's the calm that crushes chaos. Peace is the proof of power.

LAW 22

THE HOLY SPIRIT IS YOUR OPERATING SYSTEM

"...Not by might, nor by power, but by my spirit, saith the LORD of hosts."

—ZECHARIAH 4:6

God is not an app. He is not an update. He is not a patch for spiritual glitches. He is the Operating System. The Holy Spirit doesn't crash, doesn't corrupt, can't be hacked. Nor does He lag in low places or freeze under pressure and at inopportune times. He functions flawlessly...from eternity past into your present pain or problem.

In the Old Testament, when He came, He came with force:

- He rushed upon Samson, and lions lost their roars.
- He fell on Gideon, and fear folded into ferocity.

- He stirred David, and psalms poured out that still break chains today.
- He whispered to prophets, and fire fell from Heaven, seas split, armies scattered.

And then, He moved in, no longer visiting, but now indwelling. Paul asked, "What? know ye not that your body is the temple of the Holy Ghost which is in you, which ye have of God, and ye are not your own?" (1 Corinthians 6:19).

He doesn't dwell in temples made with hands—He chooses hearts made by Heaven.

The Holy Spirit is God within you. He comforts, counsels, corrects, and is a convicting force. It's what He does. He is the seal, signet, wind, whisper, and Heaven's presence in earth's vessel. It's who He is.

In the New Testament when He came, power followed:

- Peter, who once panicked before a servant girl, preached with fire, and three thousand people believed.
- Paul, who once persecuted the church, now planted them with purpose.
- Tongues of fire fell from Heaven, giving the apostles new languages they had never studied before to propel the gospel worldwide.
- Prisons shook, setting captives free.
- Demons fled on command.
- The ordinary did the extraordinary.

Not because they were trained, but because they were transformed!

He intercedes when you're too broken to pray.

He translates your tears into truth.
He gives gifts to build, not to boast.
He produces fruit to heal, not to impress.
He grieves when we go astray, not because He is angry, but because He is attached to our destiny.
Without Him…we don't have power.
Without Him…we don't have peace.
Without Him…we don't have that seal that confirms we are His (Romans 8:9).

That's not condemnation, that's clarity. Because with Him, you have comfort in chaos, direction in deserts, correction with compassion. You have access to the mind of God Himself. So, if you are feeling powerless, if you are chasing peace and finding only pain, if your system keeps crashing from overload—let me lovingly ask…

Have you downloaded the divine?
Have you welcomed the Wind?
Have you said yes to the Spirit?
He is not reserved for the religious.
He is not confined to the cathedrals.
He doesn't belong to denominations.
He belongs to those who belong to Christ.

He will not condemn you, but He will comfort you. He will not shame you, but He will shape you. He will not abandon you, but He will advocate for you.

You don't need more hustle, you need His help, and He is ready to help.

You don't need another motivational quote. You need a mover and shaker within.

And here is the beautiful mystery: He is already knocking. He is already whispering. He is already wooing. He just wants the yes. So, pause here for one moment… Breathe in the possibility…now whisper back, "Come, Holy Spirit. Fill me. Fix me. Fuel me. Function within me."

This is not emotion, my friend. This is invitation. This is not pressure. This is power. This is not tradition. This is transformation.

The Spirit…is the System. No reboot required. No upgrade necessary. Just your yes.

LAW 23

MIRACLES MOVE THROUGH MOVEMENT

"...stretch out thine hand over the sea, and divide it..."

—EXODUS 14:16

First, let's get something out of the way. It is important that you stay on point and I keep you on point here, regarding miracles.

Biblical miracles aren't random spectacles or emotional tricks. They serve four foundational purposes:

- Validate God's messenger: Each confirmed that the one speaking was sent by God.
- Usher in a new era: Miracles marked key moments of divine transition—deliverance from Egypt, the establishment of the Kingdom through Jesus, the launch of the church.
- Display God's sovereignty: Over nature, disease, death, and evil—the miracle of the feeding, the calming of the storm, resurrection...all reveal God's rule over everything.

- Fulfill prophecy: Miracles were never standalone. They were God's signs that a covenant or prophetic promise was being carried out.

This means true miracles are cohesive, purposeful, and always point beyond themselves.

Now then, let's talk about the story in John 5:1–18 (NIV), the healing at Bethesda. It provides a great illustration of how miracles move through movement. A man had been paralyzed for thirty-eight years. This was not a random illness, but rather likely rooted in soul issues like bitterness, false testimony, or other sinful habits. Jesus didn't mobilize spectacle. He spoke directly: "Get up, pick up your mat and walk" (5:8). The man had to move in order to activate the miracle. Had he opted to continue to prolong his pity party of learned helplessness and blaming others for his predicament, there would have been no miracle that day.

Understand you can not expect or look to God to do for you what you are unwilling to do for yourself, so get up! and get after it. As long as there is breath in your lungs, movement in your limbs, and you have a reasonable portion of health and strength, you have plenty. Use that, and God will take care of the rest.

Then Jesus issued a spiritual warning: "Stop sinning, or something worse may happen to you" (5:14). The miracle was real, but only part of the transformation. Spiritual surrender was required of him. Miracles reveal power, yet also call for purity.

Modern culture and many megachurches can turn miracles into commodities or manipulation tools. If it's about ratings, they will fake it. If they chase spectacle, it's often staged.

Real miracles are:

1. Coherent with Scripture, not sensational hyperbole
2. Fruit-bearing, not fundraising gimmicks
3. God-exalting, not pastor-glorifying
4. Part of a consistent storyline—not isolated spectacles

So, if you want to display this divine power and move into miracles then:

1. Obey His Word quickly. When God says, "Arise," don't hesitate, do it now. Miracles open when obedience happens.
2. Stay clean and confident. If sin binds you, confession clears the path for release.
3. Cultivate faith-fueled movement. Miracles emerge out of faith—expectant, obedient, and grounded.
4. Partner with the Holy Spirit. He directs your movement. A closed fist won't receive power; an open one will.
5. Look for the meaning. Every miracle has a message, either of repentance, revelation, or redemption.

Remember Elijah: he prayed in solitude and God's fire answered publicly (1 Kings 18). Peter stretched out his hand in faith, and salvation spread (Acts 3:1–10). Philip preached about Jesus in Samaria, and miracles confirmed his message (Acts 8:5–7). Notice that each acted with intentional obedience, not spectacle.

Miracles don't fall like confetti. They flow like fire, but only where faith fuels movement.

God didn't heal the lame man so he could lounge. He healed him so he would live. Jesus says the same to you today:

Rise...

Step out of paralysis, spiritual or practical. Move in obedience, and let God prove He is with you, for you, and in control.

Miracles move through movement. Faith without flight leads to stagnancy. But one step in faith can lead to a lifetime of wonder.

LAW 24

INTEGRITY INVITES INCREASES

"The integrity of the upright shall guide them: but the perverseness of transgressors shall destroy them."

—PROVERBS 11:3

This law is not to be confused with others already discussed. While character is your substance, and image is your presentation, integrity is something different. It has its own merit as a divine power. Integrity is your alignment. And if there is no humility, neither can be a thriving attribute of your personality.

It's the sacred beam that stitches what you believe to how you behave. It is the invisible thread that makes you whole in a world full of hollow halves. You can have character in theory, and still be inconsistent in action. You can have an image that inspires applause, but lack the interior strength to sustain it when tested.

Integrity is when the inside agrees with the outside. It's

when private loyalty matches public living. It's when you'd rather lose with truth than win with deception. It's when you'd rather have Jesus than silver and gold. That's when increases find you; you won't have to look for them.

When God went looking for a promotion candidate, He didn't pick the polished; He picked the proven. Let me provide some receipts:

- Daniel had integrity in Babylon. He wouldn't eat the king's meat, wouldn't bow to culture, wouldn't hide his prayer time, and so as a result, lions couldn't touch him and kings had to honor him.
- Joseph had integrity in Potiphar's house. He fled temptation when Potiphar's wife tried to seduce him, kept silent in the face of betrayal, interpreted dreams while forgotten, and God increased him from prisoner to prime minister.
- Ruth had integrity when it didn't pay. She stayed loyal to Naomi, gleaned the fields without fame, lived a pure life, and found her increase in the form of Boaz and a bloodline legacy to follow.

But let's be clear: Integrity is not perfection. It's direction. It's waking up and choosing again—to be honest, to be whole, to be holy, even when no one is watching, even when compromise would have been easier. You don't need to advertise integrity. God tests it, not for him but for you. And then Heaven will give its endorsement.

When your motives are aligned with your mission, when your principles are stronger than your pressure, when your soul doesn't split to fit in, you attract divine favor.

Bob Marley, who sold millions of albums as he introduced the world to reggae music, came from humble beginnings and as a young child experienced poverty as well as the confusion of racism as his father, a white man, was disowned by his family for being with his mother, a black woman. But Bob knew who he was and where he came from and summed up the essence of life in saying, "The greatness of a man is not in how much wealth he acquires, but in his integrity and his ability to affect those around him positively." He didn't pretend or fake it. His genuineness was palpable and infectious as others felt they could be themselves around him.

God can increase you without damaging others. He can elevate you without an ego boost. He can give you influence because you've proven. He can trust you with integrity. And what is meant by increase?

- It looks like doors opening that no man can shut.
- It looks like favor in rooms where you were never introduced.
- It looks like more responsibility because you handled less without cutting corners.

That is what being increased looks like. Because of your integrity, it's God leveling you up for bigger and better things.

So, check your seams, check your stitching, check what your soul is standing on when no one else is looking. Because in the Kingdom of God...promotion doesn't come from personality, it comes from purity. Not platform, but integrity.

Integrity invites your increase just as humility will receive it gracefully. It was Mother Teresa who said, "If you are humble, nothing will touch you, neither praise nor disgrace, because you know what you are."

LAW 25

FASTING FUELS FUNCTION

"And he said unto them, This kind can come forth by nothing, but by prayer and fasting."

—MARK 9:29

Fasting is not about hollow stomachs. It's about heightened spirit. It's not self-denial for drama, it's divine focus for function.

Fasting is how we turn down the noise of the flesh so we can tune in to the voice of the Father.

It is not punishment, it is preparation. Not a hunger strike, but a holy strategy.

Fasting is not ritual; it is readiness.

We have been taught to see fasting as an ancient act of religious ritual, but what if fasting is Heaven's hidden high-performance protocol? A sacred setup for bold assignments, big decisions to be made, and divine direction?

God never wastes a command. When He calls us to fast, He is not emptying us—He's equipping us.

God, in His infinite genius, wired your body to respond to fasting not with failure but with focus.

In the absence of food:

- Catecholamines—such as norepinephrine—surge, sharpening your attention and elevating alertness. Your mental fog lifts, your reaction time improves, and your discernment sharpens.
- Insulin levels drop, allowing your body to burn fat more efficiently, fueling not only your body but also clarity of thought.
- Ketone production increases. These natural fuel sources enhance memory, protect brain neurons, and stimulate creativity. Your spirit is in prayer while your brain is in power mode.
- Inflammation reduces, giving your physical frame the capacity to endure, not just emotionally, but biologically.
- Autophagy is activated. Your body begins cellular repair, clearing out damaged parts and making room for new growth. The body is literally renewing itself while the Spirit is realigning itself with God's purpose and plan for you.

So, when your plate is empty, your purpose is getting prepped. When your stomach grumbles, your soul starts to sing.

For Moses, fasting preceded revelation. He fasted forty days and nights on Mt. Sinai. No bread. No water. Yet his face glowed with glory not from sunlight but from the Son's light. He returned not gaunt with weakness. He returned with the Ten Commandments, Heaven's policy printed on stone. Fasting didn't drain him; it downloaded destiny (Exodus 34:28).

David fasted for healing, fasted for grief, fasted in repentance. His life proves that when your soul is shaken, fasting stabilizes what tears can't.

Anna the Prophetess was an eighty-four-year-old widow, fasting day and night in the temple, waiting for the Messiah. She became the first prophet to confirm the Christ Child (Luke 2:36–38). Fasting makes you see what others miss.

Before commissioning Paul and Barnabas, the leaders of the church in Antioch fasted. They didn't want to just send men. They wanted to send the right men. Fasting clears static so we can hear God speak specifics.

A word of caution—Jesus warned us in Matthew 6 not to fast like the Pharisees with disfigured faces and dramatic gestures because we are not performers on a stage. Fasting is not a performance, it's a posture. Not for Instagram, but for intimacy. "But when you fast, put oil on your head and wash your face… but only to your Father, who is unseen; and your Father, who sees what is done in secret, will reward you" Matthew 6:17-18.

Real power doesn't parade. It is dressed in silence. It is oiled in reverence. It is tucked away, and explodes at the appointed time.

Fasting is truly a divine power that we have at our disposal. Therefore…

- fast when you are facing a major decision;
- fast to break patterns, not just for deliverance, but for discernment;
- fast before new seasons, ministries, moves, marriages; and
- fast to humble the soul and awaken the spirit.

You can not feed the flesh and fuel the spirit at the same time. Some mountains remain until you make room. Some answers stay clouded until your appetite shifts from food to fellowship with the Father. Some victories hide behind the veil of hunger.

Fasting doesn't weaken you, it weaponizes you. It is not starvation, it is a soul strategy for success.

Now my question to you is: are you ready to employ this divine power and move the mountains in your life? Start by moving your plate.

LAW 26

UNITY MULTIPLIES POWER

"...how pleasant it is for brethren to dwell together in unity!"

—PSALM 133:1

In the book of Amos, the question is asked, "Can two walk together, unless they agree?" (3:3). We are also reminded in Ecclesiastes that "a three-stranded cord is not quickly broken" (4:12). Both statements speak of unity.

Unity isn't just a nice thing to have; it's necessary. It turns personal power into colossal influence. Walking in unity requires agreement of purpose. Not every step, but every direction is agreed upon. One strand will break under pressure, two fray by friction, but three? Now that knits into resilient strength.

As you think about unity, be it at home or work or in your community, consider these things:

- Clarify the common vision. Ask the question: what are we building together? Only a unified vision will empower a unified movement.
- Engage in shared responsibility. Distribute roles and avoid dictating tasks because real unity is built on shared sweat, not just shared seats.
- Cultivate conflict with care. In a cord, strands press each other; there is some tension. But the friction strengthens. Safe disagreement, committed reconciliation, now that's unity in action.
- Celebrate the collective, not just individual wins. Loud systems scream out, "I did it!" United ones will say, "We did it!" That culture will shift from combative to collaborative.

The Musketeers weren't paragons of perfection, but they were proof that when individuals bind their hearts to a shared purpose, they multiply their power beyond what any lone hero could muster. With that understanding, we still say today what they said centuries ago: "All for one, and one for all."

Unity transforms tasks into triumphs.

Let's take this divine power even further.

In the symphony of Scripture and the sanctuary of sound doctrine, no illustration of unity pulses with more divine clarity than the Trinity: Father, Son, and Holy Spirit. Three distinct persons. One indivisible God. The most sacred mystery of mutual submission and divine synchronization. The Godhead doesn't compete, it cooperates. It doesn't fracture, it flows. It doesn't jostle for rank or recognition, it rejoices in perfect alignment.

The Father reigns in eternal sovereignty, being holy, omniscient, and omnipresent. The Son radiates the visible image of the invisible God, in flesh amongst us. The Spirit rushes into the void, fills believers, and guides the godly with whispers of eternal wisdom. The unity of the Godhead is not cosmetic, it's cosmic.

If the Father is the architect, and the Son the bridge, then the Holy Spirit is the wind beneath the wings of the redeemed, carrying out the will of God with flawless fidelity.

For without the Son, we would only behold God in anthropomorphic allegory, unreachable, unrelatable, and unspeakably holy. But the Logos put on limbs, wrapped Himself in ribcage and breath, and made His dwelling amongst us.

He touched the leper.

He wept at Lazarus's tomb.

He walked dusty roads with dirty feet, and carried a bloodstained cross on borrowed shoulders.

And yet, He said, "It is better for you that I go away" (John 16:7 GNT). Because in leaving, He wasn't abandoning us, He was equipping us.

The Holy Spirit descended, not just upon, but within us. No longer tabernacled in tents or temples made by men, but housed in hearts. He brought with him not goosebumps, but governance. Not just a chill, but conviction, clarity, and comfort.

For who knows the mind of God? Only the Spirit of God. And we, frail though we are, have been gifted that same Spirit to dwell within us. What divine democracy! What scandalous grace!

Now we come to the church, bruised but blood-bought, battered but beloved is His body. And this body has many members. Eyes that see injustice. Hands that feed the hungry. Feet that bring good news. Minds that discern truth. Hearts that house compassion. But, the body cannot bless while it bickers. It cannot conquer while it competes. It can not heal while it hates itself.

Yet if the body ever awakened in unified expression, if the lungs of the church inhale the breath of God again, and exhale as one voice into the earth, then systems would shift, nations would notice, and hell would panic.

Unity isn't just a side-note in divine theology, it's the mechanism of manifestation. If the trinity is one—and Christ prayed that we be one—then we are never more like Heaven than when we walk in lockstep as one church, with one Christ and one cause. "That they all may be one; as thou, Father are in me, and I in thee, that they also may be one in us…" (John 17:21).

The prayer has already been prayed, the power has already been given. What remains…is our response.

So rise, body of Christ. Rise, reader of this revelation. Let the law of unity reawaken your divine identity.

You are not alone. You were never meant to be alone. And when we walk together, not in competition, but in covenant, we multiply a power that cannot be ignored. We shall be that city that sits upon a hill, which becomes the light unto the world (Matthew 5:14).

LAW 27

FORGIVENESS FREES THE FLOW

"...even as Christ forgave you, so also do ye."

—COLOSSIANS 3:13

Unforgiveness is spiritual constipation. You are filled with waste. You can't release what Heaven gave you when you are clogged with bitterness. Jesus said that if you don't forgive, neither will the Father forgive you (Matthew 6:15).

Greene says hold grudges, crush enemies. God says to forgive…seventy times seven. Forgiveness isn't weakness, it's warfare. You must be willing to let go so that God can let loose in your life.

We all can think of that one time when we felt betrayed by someone we trusted. Lied on by someone we were loyal to, deceived by that person who you thought was your ride or die for life. And it truly leaves a bitter taste in your mouth. You are reluctant to expose your heart again, reluctant to allow anyone to get close. They have gone on with their life, but you are all but done with people. You are in prison, shackling your feelings, mind, and heart to a thing called unforgiveness. Again, most of us, if we have lived any significant time, have crossed this path, but we don't have to and can not afford to stay on this path. You will find out that it's a next-level power to forgive, truly forgive. It is not a power you can muster up on your own, but one that needs a source stronger than you, a divine source, to help you forgive and let go and let your heart soften and your mind be sharpened by the things gained when you forgive.

"I came here today to forgive you."

Those were the words Warrick Dunn, a former NFL Pro Bowler running back, son, and sudden head of the household, spoke to the man who murdered his mother. At just eighteen years old, Dunn had to bury his mom, Betty Smothers, a police officer who was shot and killed in the line of duty. He had to divide football dreams for fatherly duties. As the oldest with five younger siblings, he, with the help of his grandmother, raised them while carrying a pain few could comprehend. But years later, in Angola Prison, standing face to face with Kevan Brumfield, his mother's killer, Dunn chose not rage or revenge, but release.

"You've taken so much of my life away from me that I want it back," he said. And with that he reclaimed more than his time; he reclaimed peace. That forgiveness wasn't just for the killer, it was for Dunn.

Dunn went on to say, "I forgave him. Then I went to my mom's grave and said…Mom, I've let it go."

That is what divine power looks like. Not noise, not payback. Just a man filled with God enough to say, "I release you, so that I can rise."

He rose for the legacy of a mother whose badge as an officer of the law couldn't save her. However, her son's grace saved hundreds of single mothers who were struggling to have homes through his charity, where he built homes for them. He established a place for them and their children to live in honor of his mother.

Forgiveness set him free. Free to reframe, realign, and not allow his mother's work and name to be buried in bitterness. Rather, it became a monument of hope to other single mothers in similar circumstances.

Whatever you might be carrying, not letting go of, or wishing bad on a person who wounded you, it is time. Time to let it go. It's a process, but it's time to begin that process so that you can finally blossom into your purpose and turn this wrong into a right for you. It's time to be a blessing to yourself and others in your circle who have seen you carry this pain and have been in pain with you. Let it go so you can be free.

It has been said that forgiveness is to set the prisoner free and realize that the prisoner is you.

> *Forgiveness is a freedom key, unlocking souls from misery.*
> *Not a pardon for the pain, but peace*
>   *that pours like healing rain.*
> *You're not excusing what they've done, you're*
>   *choosing light over the gun.*
> *You're trading shackles for release, letting bitter bondage cease.*
> *To carry wrath is weight and rust, it slows*
>   *the process, betrays the just.*
> *The past, when held too tight, will choke the*
>   *very dreams you thought you spoke.*
> *So lay aside that heavy yoke, let mercy*
>   *breathe, let judgment soak.*
> *The cross was proof of love divine, forgiveness is a holy sign.*

It doesn't mean you must forget, but heal
 the wound, not feed regret.
It's not for them, it's for you, to walk in grace and power too.
So drop the grudge, let vengeance go, and
 feel the Spirit start to flow.
No longer stuck, you now press on anew,
 because the weight is gone...
The chains are gone, too.

LAW 28

JOY STABILIZES FUNCTION

"...the joy of the LORD is your strength."

—NEHEMIAH 8:10

Let's get this out of the way. I am not talking about being happy or happiness. It's good to have it, and experience it, but it is not joy. Happiness hinges on happening. It's momentary. Mood-based. Fleeting.

Joy, however, is anchored in eternity. It doesn't flinch in affliction. It doesn't evaporate under pressure. Joy is the internal thermostat that governs external climate. While happiness reacts, joy rules. Where there is no joy, there will be no consistency in function, primarily because you don't like what you are doing. You find no reason or purpose or satisfaction. Ever felt that way about a thing?

But where joy overflows, there is resilience, rhythm, and renewal.

Let's talk about a story of resilience and renewal.

Nehemiah, a cupbearer turned builder, had just led the people of Jerusalem in the rebuilding of the city walls, which were a symbol of protection, dignity, and divine covering. After years of vulnerability, shame, and exile, the walls were again up, but their hearts still needed repair.

So Nehemiah, together with the priest Ezra, gathered the people not to celebrate their physical achievement, but to rebuild their spiritual foundation.

We find in Nehemiah 8, Ezra standing on a wooden platform before a sea of people—men, women, and even children old enough to understand. For hours, he reads from the book of the law of Moses. As the words echo through the air, something begins to shift. The people aren't cheering. They aren't shouting in triumphant victory. They are weeping, yes…they are crying. Because for the first time in generations, they heard the truth. They realized how far they had drifted. They mourned their disobedience. They lamented the years lost in compromise. They realized the reason they had lost the war to the Babylonians—who breached the city's walls, burned down the gates, and took the citizens captive—was not because of their physical impotence. They knew that they had become spiritually weak, and their malnourished souls made them powerless physically. It's a hard pill to swallow when one sees the error of one's ways. This weeping wasn't empty emotionalism, it was conviction. It hit different. It rocked their souls.

But just when it seems this will become a day of wailing, sorrow, and shame, Nehemiah interrupts their weeping with a divine directive: "This day is holy unto the LORD your God. Do not mourn or weep" (Nehemiah 8:9 NIV). And then the famous line: "Go and enjoy choice food and sweet drinks, and send some to those who have nothing prepared. This day is holy to our Lord. Do not grieve, for the joy of the LORD is your strength" (Nehemiah 8:10 NIV).

Nehemiah isn't downplaying their conviction, he is reframing it. Their tears were proof that their hearts were soft again. They were no longer dull, deceived, or distracted listeners. They were now devoted to listening to the Word of God. Their grief meant the Word was working, and now it was time to exchange sorrow for strength. Notice, Nehemiah didn't say, "Your joy is your strength." He said the Lord's joy is in bringing strength to you.

You see, it wasn't their celebration that empowered them. It was God's delight in their return. The same God who was grieved by their rebellion was now glad over their restoration. And His joy, not their perfection, became their power source. And in reciprocity, they also had joy in the Lord. We love Him because He first loved us.

A thorough understanding of this context enables us to make an accurate application. This context is functional.

- Conviction precedes their power surge.
- The Word brought clarity and course correction.
- When they returned to God, His joy became their fuel.
- God's joy becomes your joy.

So today, right now, if you're broken, inconsistent, weeping over your missteps, beating yourself up over your bad decisions, don't stay stuck in grief.

Get back into the Word and let the two-edged sword cut you. Let it open you. Let it operate on your mind and soul. Let it heal you. Let it bring you home. Then, receive the smile of the Savior and move forward in His joy.

You can have joy. You can rise and be successful and get

back on track. It's not a road of drudgery. It can be an enjoyable journey because every bump, pothole, and detour helps get you to this point of realizing the need to level up.

Robert Greene does something sly in *The 48 Laws of Power*. He warns you early, subtly, surgically, that if you pursue power by any means necessary, you must relinquish your right to happiness. "Power is not happiness," he writes. In other words, expect betrayal. Expect paranoia. Expect emotional detachment as the price of dominance. It's the fine print of his entire framework. He says if you seek control, you must forfeit connection.

If you manipulate others, don't expect meaning. If you deceive to ascend, prepare to be lonely at the top.

But that's not wisdom, that's a warning from a broken paradigm. It's a truth twisted into a trap, saying: "You want power, then say goodbye to peace."

It is almost as if Greene knows that the methods he endorses—deceit, emotional manipulation, domination—will ultimately corrode the soul. So what does he do? He warns you in advance as if it's a badge of honor and convinces you to believe that this is the cost of power. And as a result, he numbs your conscience before it kicks in and tells you there is something not quite right about all this. But like a surgeon with no anesthesia, he prepares you to bleed in silence. He suggests that you can win the world and lose your soul, and not only is that okay, but it's to be expected.

Let's be clear: this does not demonstrate insight. But it has the appearance of intellectual gaslighting. And it's one of the oldest tricks of the enemy: trade the fruit of joy for the illusion of control. Like a roaring lion, in the end you will be devoured by self-consumption as you pursue the goal of having all power in Heaven and on Earth. Now that is scary. And even more scary to think that it is attainable.

Divine power doesn't deal in bargains that bankrupt the soul. In God's Kingdom, power flows through joy, not past it. Function is stabilized, not sabotaged, by a level of selfishness and power hunger that is insatiable.

Joy isn't a casualty of calling, it's evidence you're still called.

When the joy of the Lord is your strength, you don't have to fake smiles while dying on the inside. You don't have to win at the cost of wellness. You don't have to become a monster to defeat one.

You can walk in power without paranoia.

You can rise in influence without losing your integrity.

You can lead without manipulation, succeed without sadness, and serve without exhaustion. Because divine power does not sacrifice the fruit of the Spirit for fame.

Let's be clear: Joy is not optional for those who walk in divine power; it's essential. So if the blueprint you are or have been following demands that you surrender joy to maintain your place, you're not in divine dominion, you're in deception, and it's time to pivot.

The world may sell sadness as a strategy for success. But in Heaven's economy, joy is strength and a necessary currency.

Greene prepared you to settle for power that hurts. But this law invites you to stand in divine power that heals.

Joy isn't a luxury, it's a lifeline. And without it, purpose becomes heavy. But with it, function becomes fueled.

So, if you've lost your joy—go back to the well, come back to His presence, and get back into His Word, and you will know the truth and that truth will make you free.

LAW 29

EXCELLENCE EXPANDS AUTHORITY

"And whatsoever ye do, do it heartily, as to the Lord, and not unto men."

—COLOSSIANS 3:23

Excellence isn't elitist, it's inherited. It's not just about performance, it's about proximity to a perfect father. For those born of God, excellence isn't a chore, it's a characteristic. When God spoke light into darkness, it wasn't average. It wasn't adequate. It was good, and then later, it was very good. From Eden to eternity, His work has always been flawless, intentional, and complete.

So when we reflect God, we don't settle for mediocre. We mirror His magnificence.

What loving parent would raise a child and say, "Just do the bare minimum," "Try not to stand out," or "Blend in, be basic." No. A good father says, "Carry my name with weight. Reflect my worth. Show them whose child you are."

And just like your earthly last name, your spiritual legacy demands excellence. Why? Because your Father is excellent. And if we're made in His image, then we've got no business having a lackadaisical approach to anything we commit to doing. If we are going to do it, then we do it with excellence.

"By faith Abel offered to God a more excellent sacrifice than Cain…" (Hebrews 11:4). Both brothers brought something. But one brought his best, and the other brought what he had left. Abel's excellence expanded his favor, even in death. Cain's negligence and laziness shrank his influence, even in life.

It was not about God demanding perfection, but it was about being deserving of priority.

Paul understood the power of priority. He was well educated and went to the best schools and sat under the best professors. He had status and religious prestige. But he counted it all trash compared to knowing Christ: "…I count all things but loss for the excellency of the knowledge of Christ Jesus my Lord…" (Philippians 3:8). Because the highest form of excellence isn't in your intellect or your image but in your intimacy (knowing, to know) with Christ. Paul's authority expanded and his priorities shifted. The more he walked with and like his Father, the more doors opened for Heaven to use him.

Excellence isn't just for preachers and prophets. It's for mechanics, mothers, managers, medical professionals, and musicians. "And whatsoever ye do, do it heartily, as to the Lord, and not unto men, (Colossians 3:23). If your hands are on it, then Heaven should be proud of it. Because even in work, you can worship or give tribute to God, and worship without excellence is just noise, it's not music to His ears.

This divine power is all about attitude. It's all about recognizing your divine nature and allowing it to flow through you. There is nothing mediocre, or mundane, or slothful about waking up every day to embrace a new day not promised and never seen before. Your perspective will be different, uncommon, and unlike the world's, but you will stand out and stand up. As you walk in excellence, doors open without your forcing them.

Respect increases not because of your title, but because of your integrity. Influence multiplies because people trust consistency over charisma. Spiritual dominion rises because God places greater weight on those who have shown they can and will carry it well.

In other words, excellence expands your reach, your reputation, and your reign.

God has never birthed a slacker. And if excellence is your Father's fingerprint, then half-hearted work is spiritual amnesia. You simply have forgotten who you are and whose you are. Let the world recognize your parentage, not by platform, but by the power and precision of how you live, love, lead, and labor. So let excellence flow from your spirit, and with that, authority will flow as well.

LAW 30

COMPASSION IS DIVINE CURRENCY

"...be ye kind one to another..."

—EPHESIANS 4:32

We should spend compassion generously because it was first spent on us.

In fact, you are still here, not because you have been so perfect, but because God's compassion gave you another morning. Before your alarm clock sounded, He renewed His mercy (Lamentations 3:22–23). That's not coincidence, my friend, that's currency.

We talk about second chances like we deserve them. We don't. But God gives them anyway—not because we earned them but because He is compassionate.

Every new day is an unpaid invoice stamped "Grace Covered." And we are called not to hoard it, but to distribute it as well.

Money can buy access. Fame can buy applause. But only compassion can buy credibility that lasts in God's economy.

People don't follow titles, they follow tenderness. They aren't moved by your position, but by your posture. They will forget your sermon, but will never forget your embrace. Compassion is how God invests in us…and how we invest in others.

In Matthew 18, Jesus tells a man forgiven of a massive debt he could never repay that the master canceled it. He has a clean slate. But what does the man do? He turns right around and grabs a fellow servant by the neck, demanding repayment of a small debt owed, and, when the servant can't pay, he has the servant thrown in jail. Jesus does not just call this wicked, He called it unforgivable. Because when you receive compassion, the expectation is that you will reflect it. To withhold compassion after being flooded with it from Heaven is spiritual fraud.

Now let's be honest, compassion isn't natural. It requires emotional maturity, ego management, and a good memory of how far God has brought you.

You don't wake up with this divine power. It has to be cultivated and reflected upon. It takes time to look past people's behavior and see their burden. It takes patience to sit in someone else's sorrow without trying to fix it. It takes power to feel pain that isn't yours and still act on it.

For example, Greene advises readers to avoid the unhappy and the unlucky. In other words, don't linger around people in this state—he claims they will slow you down, impede your productivity, and poison your goals. To him, empathy is a liability and compassion is an inefficient use of energy. He pushes for a stoic detachment: don't feel, suppress your emotions, because feelings only fester in ignorance anyway.

But such views are damaging.

Psychologists know well that chronic emotional suppression

breeds burnout and mental strain, that cutting empathy disconnects you from reality and weakens the very relationships and team morale that sustain true progress. Manipulation erodes trust—first with others, then within yourself. And mobility without meaning, no matter how fast it moves, often ends in the hollow shell of success, isolated and empty.

When we seek to become careless and ruthless in pursuit of power, it is a moral decline. Perhaps it starts with being ruthless with coworkers. But then it progresses to emotional detachment with friends.

Ultimately family bonds are destroyed. Your own nucleus is disrupted, and a mutated cell becomes cancerous.

Divine power of compassion offers a better way. Jesus wept at Lazarus's tomb—compassion didn't deplete Him, it displayed His deity. Paul urged kindness and patience—as fruit of the Spirit. True authority isn't ruthless—it's relational.

You can still stand strong and, at the same time, feel deeply. You can still lead, but love strong.

So, ask yourself: Do you want power that alienates, or power that amplifies souls? Do you want ruthless manipulation, or radical compassion? Do you want temporary control, or transformational influence?

Heaven's power play tilts wholeheartedly toward the divine power of compassion.

Chuck Feeney, the billionaire behind Duty Free Shoppers (DFS), made billions and secretly gave nearly all of it away. No spotlights, no stadium dedications. No flashy foundations. He said, "It is a lot more fun giving while you're alive than giving when you're dead."

He was able to become a billionaire without following a dark triad of narcissistic (all about self) views, showing signs of psychopathy, or having a Machiavellian approach towards others. In fact, he was known for living in a rented apartment, flying coach, and wearing a fifteen-dollar watch. He gave not from guilt, but from grace. Not for clout, but out of conviction. Nor did he lose his joy in the process. He said giving was fun and exciting. He had joy in giving.

Now imagine a world where more people had power but didn't flaunt it, had resources but didn't hoard them, and had compassion and used it as currency. That is divine economics!

Compassion didn't originate in philanthropy. It began at Calvary. The cross is the most extravagant act of compassion this world has ever seen or known. And the same God who looked on the multitudes with compassion (Matthew 9:36) now expects His people to do the same. When Jesus wept at Lazarus's tomb, it wasn't because He couldn't fix it. It was because He felt it. That's compassion: the ability to feel the ache…even when you hold the answer.

Compassion isn't weakness. It's wisdom with warmth. It's Kingdom currency that never loses its value. And the more you spend it, the more you are trusted with. Because Heaven's math says—he who sows mercy reaps influence, he who weeps with others, walks in power, and he who gives like God, lives like God.

LAW 31

TIMING TRUMPS TALENT

"...there is a season, and a time to every purpose under the heaven."
—ECCLESIASTES 3:1

Time is not your enemy. It's God's instrument.

We often worship the gifts, the grit, and the grind. But in God's Kingdom, it's not just about the grind, it's also about the gliding into His timing. You can be gifted but not greenlit. Talented but untimely. Brilliant, yet blocked. Not because you lack purpose, but because you lack placement in God's plan.

"The race is not to the swift, nor the battle to the strong...but time and chance happeneth to them all."
—ECCLESIASTES 9:11

Talent may open doors, but only timing opens destiny.

To understand divine timing, one must first stand in awe of

divine sovereignty. God exists outside of time, yet orchestrates everything within it. He's not watching history unfold—He's writing it.

He doesn't rush. He doesn't delay. He's never early. Never late. Always on time.

Now here is where I must confront a mystery regarding those deep waters of human freedom (free will) and foreknowledge.

If God already knows what will happen, do we even have free will? The answer is yes! God's foreknowledge doesn't negate your free will; it simply navigates through it. In other words, He doesn't force your decisions. He factors them in. Look at it this way: a GPS doesn't force you to follow the route, but it can recalculate every wrong turn to still get you home! That's God. He knows you will fall from time to time and has already placed grace on the map!

Let's go back to Egypt. God promised the Hebrews a land flowing with milk and honey. But He didn't say how long it would take. Why? Because promise is one thing. Preparation is another.

Their years in the wilderness weren't just about testing their faith, it was about timing their entry. "Ye have compassed this mountain long enough: turn you northward" (Deuteronomy 2:3). He used the wilderness as a filter: to let the doubters die off and the devoted come to the forefront. It wasn't about their skill or talent. It was about their season.

God moves you forward not when you're strong but when you're ready.

Joseph had dreams, but dreams need deadlines. So, God allowed the betrayal, the pit, the prison. Because He already saw that there was famine on the horizon and Joseph had to be positioned to preserve life—not only his, but the twelve tribes of Jacob (Israel) as well. Genesis 50:20 explains that what was meant for evil, God meant for good...to save many lives.

God timed the famine and planted a man in Pharaoh's court, choosing not the man who was smartest, but the one who was the most surrendered.

Regarding Jesus, "...when the fulness of the time was come, God sent forth his Son..." (Galatians 4:4). He didn't come during the Tower of Babel, nor did he come during Babylon's empire, or during Egypt's dominion. He came when the roads were built, when the Greek language unified the trade, when Rome's Pax Romana (a period of Roman peace lasting two hundred years) made the gospel portable. Not a second too soon, and not a minute too late, but in the fullness of time God sent his son!

When the Jews rejected Jesus, the door swung open to the Gentiles. Romans 11 teaches us that God uses rejection as a means of redirection. The Gentiles didn't sneak in; they were grafted in by God Himself. Salvation isn't a free-for-all, per se—it's a timed unveiling, and in perfect timing, there will be that moment when the time of the Gentiles has come (or is up) and that door will be closed. "For I would not, brethren, that ye should be ignorant of this mystery, lest ye should be wise in your own conceits; that blindness in part is happened to Israel, until the fulness of the Gentiles be come in" (Romans 11:25).

God's delays are never wasted; they are weighted. They prepare the platform for the greatest redemption arcs throughout history.

So maybe you are frustrated, to the point where you call yourself Ms. Cantgetright, or Mr. Missedopportunity, and it feels like you're falling behind. You think, you aren't getting any younger and soon will be out of time. Well...stop clock-watching. Remember, God isn't just developing your talent and preparing your readiness. He is syncing you to Kingdom time.

Because if you get there early, you will fail. And if you arrive too late, you'll miss it. But if you move with Him, you'll thrive.

So just trust the timekeeper. God is not only the creator of time. He is the keeper of your time. He has plans for you—plans to prosper you and not harm you...but not all at once. Step by step. Season by season. So, don't rush the seed. Don't force the fruit. Rest in His rhythm. Because while men chase moments, the mature learn to wait on the movement of God.

LAW 32

BLESSING FOLLOWS BOUNDARIES

"...like a city that is broken down, and without walls."
—PROVERBS 25:28

Without boundaries, even blessings become burdens.

We live in a culture that idolizes boundary-less living. "Do you!" "Live free!" "Follow your heart!" "Walk in your own truth." But my friend, an unguarded heart becomes a target-rich environment for chaos. Freedom without fences isn't liberation—it's lawlessness. It is like driving a car with no brakes—thrilling... no doubt, until you crash, then it's not. "Keep thy heart with all diligence; for out of it are the issues of life" (Proverbs 4:23). Guard it. Fence it. Protect it. Because what flows out of your life depends on what you allow in it.

Your mother says, "Don't play in the street." Not because she is cruel. But because she loves you more than your craving for freedom. The fence wasn't punishment; it was protection. The yard wasn't a prison; it was providence.

And so it is with God. His "thou shall nots" are not denial, they're divine preservation.

- Don't worship other gods…because false gods can't love you back.
- Don't serve money…because money makes a poor master a brutal taskmaster.
- Don't seek revenge…because it poisons the vessel that carries it.
- Don't live unrestrained and undisciplined…because a man of many companions may come to ruin (Proverbs 18:24).

We can think of boundaries in terms of tiers. First, you set boundaries with yourself. This means setting internal limits to preserve your soul. For example, you should limit your intake of food, alcohol, noise, drama, and overstimulation. Protect your rest. Prioritize your peace. Learn to say no to others so you can say yes to God.

Then, you set boundaries with others.

Toxic people don't just drain energy, they disrupt your divine rhythm. If you can not redirect them, then it's not their season to change—nor is it yours to change them. It's time to let them go. Scripture warns us, "Be not deceived: evil communications corrupt good manners" (1 Corinthians 15:33).

Remember, distance isn't disrespect, it's discernment. Jesus loved everyone…but He didn't let everyone in his inner circle.

To say, "I do things my own way," is to forfeit peace at the altar of pride. You may still breathe, but you won't blossom. You may still move but you will always meander. Because blessings flow along borders, like water through a riverbank.

God doesn't bless confusion. God doesn't bless rebellion. God blesses order, obedience, and honor.

Even the Promised Land had property lines. Tribes had designated inheritance. Boundaries created peace, unity, and sustainability.

And even in Eden, the very birthplace of paradise, God said, "'Of every tree of the garden thou mayest freely eat...'" (Genesis 2:16). But He also said there was one tree they could not eat from. Boundaries were the first divine instruction, and breaking them was the first human downfall.

So, thank God for every "no" that saved you:

- No, you can not go there.
- No, that person isn't for you.
- No, that door didn't open because the trap was set behind it.

Some of God's greatest blessings come wrapped in rejection, not promotion.

Remember, the boundary is where blessings begin. To respect them tells Heaven that you are ready for more, and it tells hell you have no access here. It also tells your future that you are making room for it, the right way. Although the yard may feel small, inside it...is safety, strength, and supernatural favor. And the child who honors the boundaries will soon grow into the one God can trust with even greater territory.

LAW 33

LISTENING POSITIONS YOU FOR LAUNCH

"Speak; for thy servant heareth."

—1 SAMUEL 3:10

The loudest one in the room isn't always the leader—sometimes it's the one least likely to hear from Heaven.

Because real power doesn't start with speaking. It starts with silence. With surrender. With stillness. Before there is a roar, there must be a reverent ear.

The wise preacher said it: "God is in heaven…you are on earth…let your words be few" (Ecclesiastes 5:2 NIV). Not because words don't matter—but because listening is the language of the launched.

In Scripture, God never releases a mantle without first revealing a message. There's always a whisper before the warfare, a command before the commission.

Samuel didn't feel his call—he heard it in the dark. Moses

didn't imagine his mission—he heard it from a burning bush. Mary didn't dream up the incarnation—she listened to Gabriel speak life into her womb.

Divine strategy doesn't float on vibes. It rides on revelation. And revelation only reaches those with spiritual ears. Revelation 2:7 states, "He that hath an ear, let him hear what the Spirit saith unto the churches..." Because how you hear determines how you're launched.

Let's be clear: listening is not a passive activity. It is a sacred discipline. A battlefield posture. A pre-launch checklist for your assignment.

Too many people hear with flesh, not with faith. They listen to respond, not to receive. To argue, not to align. To react, not to obey.

And the result? Wasted years. Wandering paths. Doors missed. Distractions married. You will never launch well if you don't listen first.

Jesus said it with holy precision: "...take heed how you hear..." (Luke 8:18 NKJV). Because listening is more than what enters your ears, it's how your spirit interprets divine instruction.

- Peter listened to Jesus say, Cast your net on the other side—and stepped into overflow.
- Elijah tuned out wind, fire, and earthquake—only the still, small voice had the map to his next mission.
- "Then the Spirit said unto Philip, Go near and join thyself to this chariot"—and one moment of obedience led to the first African conversion recorded in Acts 8:29.

In every case, the miracle moved on the back of the message heard.

Let me give you a noteworthy example of the quiet power of a man who listened. George Washington Carver, born into slavery, rose to become a groundbreaking scientist and inventor at Tuskegee Institute. He didn't chase applause—he chased the Almighty. He didn't flex for fame—he fixed his ear toward the Father.

In the stillness of the early morning, before the world awoke, Carver went into the woods not to speak, but to listen. He tuned his heart like a radio dial, adjusting the static of self until the frequency of Heaven came through clear. "Show me the mystery of the peanut," he prayed—not for patents, not for platforms, but because he had trained his ear to catch even the whisper of God's instruction.

And God spoke—not with thunder, but with threads of revelation woven into his listening spirit. Over three hundred uses flowed through that surrendered soul, not because Carver talked more, but because he listened deeper. The world saw a scientist. Heaven saw a son whose ears were anointed for insight. Divine power flowed through him not by performance but by posture, not by noise but by noticing, not by speeches but by silence that made room for God's sound.

That's what happens when you don't let the crowd create your calling—you let the voice of God carve it into your soul.

Listening is a posture of humility. It's a tool of alignment. It's a strategy of spiritual survival.

We're in a world that rewards noise. Louder equals leader. Sharper equals smarter. But Heaven does not honor hype—it honors humility.

And humility listens. Before you post, pray. Before you preach, pause. Before you lead, lean in.

You don't have to have all the answers—just the right antenna.

So listen. Not to be polite. But to prepare. To discern. To respond with precision.

Ask yourself:

- Are you waiting to speak, or waiting to hear?
- Are you tuned in to culture, or tuned up to Christ?
- Are you seeking commands—or just confirmations?

Because in the Kingdom, launch always follows listening. And when your spirit is positioned, your feet will know exactly when—and where—to go.

LAW 34

HONOR ACTIVATES HEAVEN

"Honour the LORD with thy substance, and with the firstfruits of all thine increase."

—PROVERBS 3:9

Honor is not merely a matter of character in public. It's not merely integrity in decision-making. And it's not confined to moral alignment.

Those are noble. But honor…

Honor is what you give—even when the other person doesn't deserve it. Honor is how you elevate others—because of your reverence for God's structure. Honor is how Heaven recognizes your humility.

Integrity is how you stand. It's doing right when it costs you.

Character is how you live. It's who you are when no one sees.

But Honor is how you lift—and what unlocks for you in return.

Honor is the esteem you show others and the divine order. It determines your interactions...and your access. Honor is a command tied to longevity. A divine reward system is triggered. "Honor your father and your mother...that your days may be long..." (Exodus 20:12 ESV).

God reciprocates honor. He keeps score of your reverence: "...for them that honour me I will honour, and they that despise me shall be lightly esteemed" (1 Samuel 2:30).

Dishonor disables the miraculous. Even Jesus was restricted by a culture of contempt. Jesus could do no mighty work there... because they did not honor Him (Mark 6:4–6).

Honor is a law of divine access.

Not because God is egotistical...

But because He guards His glory with principles, not preference.

You can't receive what you resent. You won't glean from what you grumble against. You'll never rise under a mantle you mock.

Honor activated the heavens over Him.

Honor God above all. Not just in worship, but in priorities, decisions, and stewardship. Honor people. Not because they're perfect—but because they carry potential. Honor your own assignment. Treat it like it came from Heaven—because it did.

Honor time. Redeem it. Don't waste what you can never get back. Honor your body. It is the temple of divine function.

If you're constantly bumping up against invisible ceilings, if the miraculous seems to elude you, if wisdom is rarely received when you speak...check your honor.

Because honor is Heaven's hearing aid. When you walk in it, speak in it, and give it freely—Heaven moves. Angels are dispatched. Grace floods in.

If integrity without honor makes you stiff, and character

without honor makes you arrogant, then honor must be the oil that makes all other virtues operate in the Spirit.

Honor isn't extra. It's essential. Because what you refuse to honor, you will eventually violate. It will only be a matter of time, so give honor to whom honor is due, and that starts with honoring yourself.

LAW 35

REST IS A RENEWAL STRATEGY

"...Come ye yourselves apart into a desert place, and rest a while..."
—MARK 6:31

In the laboratory of life, hustle may win applause—but rest is what brings repair, rhythm, and revelation.

This law doesn't encourage laziness. It authorizes longevity. It gives divine license to pause, so you can pivot with power.

Because even divine vessels need divine rhythms—for the body, the brain, and the soul.

God, the infinite, omnipotent, omniscient Creator rested.

Not because He was tired, but because He was done.

He modeled a rhythm, not mandated a ritual.

So, if the Divine Designer built in the need to cease, why do we treat rest as if it's a flaw?

In truth, it's one of the most faithful things we can do.

But God's command to rest is not just spiritual—it's physiological.

Your brain and body were wired to restore—not run endlessly.

Here's what happens when you honor the sleep cycle God programmed into your biology:

1. REM SLEEP—THE MIND'S MAINTENANCE MODE

Rapid eye movement (REM) sleep occurs multiple times per night, with increasing duration in later cycles. It's vital for emotional balance, memory consolidation, and mental clarity. It helps process spiritual insight, emotional stress, and even unresolved trauma. It's when the soul begins to breathe and the mind begins to see.

2. DELTA SLEEP—DEEP REPAIR MODE

Delta waves emerge in stage three of non-REM sleep, the most restorative part of the cycle. Cellular regeneration, tissue growth, and immune restoration occur here. HGH (human growth hormone) is secreted—essential for physical repair and vitality. Miss this stage, and you may still be "asleep," but you're not being renewed.

3. ALPHA BRAIN WAVES—GOD'S WHISPER ZONE

In restful wakefulness or early sleep, alpha waves (8–13 Hz) quiet the chaos. This is the zone where divine downloads can be heard: ideas, answers, clarity, peace. It's a powerful time for prayer, meditation, reflection, and revelation. Jesus often withdrew early in the morning or late at night to pray—and we now know the brain is most receptive to divine impressions in those alpha-rich times.

Chronic stress and sleep deprivation elevate cortisol, a hormone that can disrupt blood pressure, glucose metabolism, and even memory. Consistent rest helps lower cortisol levels and restore the hypothalamic-pituitary-adrenal (HPA) axis, allowing your body to function optimally. With cortisol calmed, creative and spiritual clarity returns—you begin to hear God again.

Rest is both a spiritual mandate and a medical necessity. God told Elijah: "Arise and eat; because the journey is too great for thee" (1 Kings 19:7). Before Elijah could prophesy again, he had to sleep again. God did not scold him for burnout—He gave him bread, water, and sleep. Even the Son of God—Jesus—slept during storms, rested on mountains, and said "Come unto Me...and I will give you rest" (Matthew 11:28).

Rest is also a form of stewardship.

Paul writes in Corinthians, "...know ye not that your body is the temple of the Holy Ghost which is in you, which ye have of God..." (1 Corinthians 6:19). You wouldn't abuse the altar in the temple—So why exhaust the temple of your body? Rest isn't just for comfort. It's for consecration. It's how you honor God with your biology.

Honor seven to nine hours of sleep per night. Schedule it like you schedule meetings.

Stop the glorification of busyness. Heaven doesn't reward burnout.

Guard Sabbath rhythms—not legalistically, but lovingly.

Journal insights before bed. The mind declutters in alpha and REM states—record divine whispers.

Rest without guilt. Renewal is not a luxury—it's divine logistics.

Your soul needs a Sabbath. The body isn't blessed by burnout. The soul doesn't sing in exhaustion.

But in divine rest, your vision is renewed, your spirit is reignited, and your function is restored.

So, rest like the righteous.

Recharge like the redeemed.

Sabbath like the sanctified.

And live like a vessel that Heaven can consistently flow through.

Because even the anointed…

Even the appointed…

Even the assigned…

Need divine renewal through rest.

LAW 36

GIVE GLORY OR LOSE GRACE

"I am the LORD: that is my name: and my glory will I not give to another..."

—ISAIAH 42:8

He is God. Period. Not partial. Not passive. Not possibly God. He is preeminent, perpetual, personal—the power behind the power, and the glory behind the grace.

When you forget that, you forfeit favor.

When you claim credit, you cancel covenant.

When you hog the honor, you hinder the heavens.

Because God does not share His stage with flesh!

Before function can lead to fullness, the Father demands a pause for praise.

Before power manifests in public, there must be a private parade of praise.

We're not talking about a tip-of-the-hat, casual clap of the hands. No! We're talking about a "from the rising of the sun unto the going down of the same…" kind of glory (Psalm 113:3)!

The kind of praise that doesn't just shout but shifts—that confuses the enemy and calls on the God of glory to step in.

Remember Jericho?

God gave no sword, no strategy, no siege weapons—just sound.

March. Move. Then make some noise.

And when they opened their mouths in praise…walls fell without a fight.

What if your breakthrough is buried under your silence? What if your victory is waiting for your volume? Praise isn't emotional hype—it's Heaven's hammer that brings down hellish strongholds.

Praise isn't about personality—it's about principle. It's not just for the loud, it's for the loyal.

Paul and Silas didn't get free until they praised.

Jehoshaphat's enemies turned on each other when the praisers marched ahead of the army.

David danced out of his dignity—and into divine destiny.

Glory is the gateway to grace, and praise is the password to power.

Scripture doesn't say God visits the praise of His people. It says He inhabits it. He doesn't pass through—He takes up residence (Psalm 22:3).

Your house becomes His house. Your mouth becomes His microphone. Your problems become His platform.

If you want God to step in, you've got to lift Him up. If you want grace to remain, you must give glory reign.

Let the spotlight land where it belongs. You didn't heal yourself—He did. You didn't open that door—He did. You didn't survive the storm—He silenced the waves.

You didn't fix your mind—He renewed it. You didn't beat the addiction—He broke the yoke.

Don't dare take what belongs to God and try to pin it to your pride. That's not just misattribution—that's misappropriation of majesty.

That's not just poor posture—that's spiritual theft.

You can have the title, the tools, the training—but if you don't give glory, you'll lose grace.

Ask Nebuchadnezzar—one minute praising himself, next minute chewing cud with cattle.

Ask Herod—cloaked in kingly garments, but consumed by worms.

Ask Lucifer—once Heaven's top worship leader, now hell's top resident.

God resists the proud, and He doesn't just walk away—He shuts down the system.

Start your day with a thank you, not a to-do list.

Praise Him in the parking lot, not just the pew.

Shout Him out in the storm, not just the sunshine.

Give Him glory when it works and when it's still working.

If you're still breathing, He's still worthy.

If you've got grace, give back glory.

If you've got favor, flood it with faithful praise.

This is the final law of function.

And before we step into fullness, we must get one thing clear:

We are not the source. We are the servants.

We are not the fire. We are the flint.

We are not the glory. We are the glass that reflects it.

And when we reflect it right…the heavens open,

the oil flows, and the power of God pours into every dry place in your life.

So, lift up your heads, O ye gates...
Open your mouth like a trumpet...
And give Him what He alone deserves:
Glory! Honor! Majesty! Power!

Because when praise goes up...grace doesn't just come down—it takes over.

Give glory...or lose grace.

The choice is yours.

PART II SUMMARY

You've walked the sacred corridors of Foundation—laid low before rising high. But now, in this second act of power's performance, you've shifted from pillars to propulsion—from being grounded...to getting going.

This isn't theology for theologians, it's functionality for the faithful. And function, real divine function, is not found in hollow hustle, but in holy alignment.

You've just walked through eighteen functional laws, each dripping with divine fuel:

- Service unlocked strategy.
- Discernment guided dominion.
- Peace stood still in the presence of chaos.
- The Holy Spirit became your operating system—never crashing, always syncing. You've fasted, forgiven, and found joy that doesn't fluctuate with feelings.

You've learned that movement isn't just motion—it's miracle-making. That timing matters more than talent, and that rest is resistance in a world addicted to burnout.

You now understand:

- Excellence expands your atmosphere.
- Unity amplifies your reach.
- Integrity is the elevator.
- Compassion is your currency.
- Boundaries bless you, not bind you.
- Listening isn't a courtesy—it's a catapult.
- And if you ever forget where power flows from…Law 36 reminded you: give glory…or lose grace.

YOU ARE NO LONGER JUST AWARE OF POWER. YOU ARE ACTIVATED IN IT.

This part—Function—was never about theory. It was training. Every chapter pressed you toward practical precision. Every law pointed to how divine power flows, functions, and flourishes in real time.

These aren't just spiritual philosophies; they're spiritual technologies.

Each law is a launchpad.

Each principle is a protocol.

Each word, a weapon.

And now…you feel it.

Not just in your mind.

But in your soul, your stride, your spirit.

What Comes Next? Fullness.

You've built the Foundation. You've mastered the Function. But there's another frequency.

It's where power moves from reliable to radiant.
Where purpose becomes overflow.
Where obedience matures into outpouring.
Where you don't just know divine power…
You embody it. You extend it. You live it.
Part III is not for the faint.

It's for those ready to walk in the fullness of Christ, where divine power is no longer a choice, but the only way you breathe. Let's finish this flight. The runway to a more powerful you is before you. A smooth landing will be in His time. Then, let's walk in Fullness. Because it's not enough to be informed. You were called to be ignited.

Shall we continue? Fight off distraction, overcome procrastination; you have come too far and the enemy is trembling. So resist him and his wiles and finish.

PART III

THE FULLNESS OF DIVINE POWER

The culmination of Greene's forty-eight laws is the consolidation of personal dominance. His ideal is to reach a level where you command fear, dominate rivals, and never show weakness. His book ends with laws like assume formlessness, despise the free lunch, or discover each man's thumbscrew. Fullness to him is total and complete control with minimal moral restraint. And it's the final lie: that power, when finally perfected, means you answer to no one.

Greene says crush others. God says help carry their burdens. Greene says stand above. God says stoop and be willing to wash another's feet.

The fullness of divine power is not found in isolation but in communion. It's not always about having the highest seat at the table. True fullness is not found in dominating men but in dwelling in God and letting His Spirit dwell richly in you. When the Spirit fills you, the world can't define you. You become unstoppable, unshakable, unbreakable. Not because of dominance, but because of divine indwelling.

LAW 37

INHERITANCE IS RELEASED THROUGH INTIMACY

"If ye abide in me, and my words abide in you, ye shall ask what ye will, and it shall be done unto you."

—JOHN 15:7

In this law we don't just take possession, we step into position. We don't just read about inheritance, we reign in it.

We will have to accept this kind of love, knowing that our inheritance isn't earned, it's embraced. An inheritance is not a paycheck, it's a birthright. It's not wages from work, it's wealth from where you come from. Inheritance is not about effort, it's about intimacy. You must be a part of the family to inherit the family's fortune. And while this world scrambles for position and posturing, the Kingdom calls us to abide, not achieve. Remain, not rush. Connect, not complete. For our abiding is in Him. We remain in the family because we are sealed into it. We are forever connected because He who began a good work in us will complete the work He started in us (Philippians 1:6).

Jesus said, "Abide in me, and I in you...for without me ye can do nothing" (John 15:4–5). At least nothing lasting, nothing life-giving, nothing worthy of the weight of Heaven's inheritance.

Intimacy with the Father isn't just about feeling close, it's about walking in covenant, legally authorized to receive what's been spiritually set aside just for you. That is why He said you must be born again, not of bloodline, but of Spirit (John 3:3–5). Not from flesh, but by faith. Not through manipulation, but by adoption. Because only the sons and daughters have access to the inheritance.

You see, it's the King's kids who get the keys to the Kingdom. Earthly fathers store up treasure to secure their children's future. How much more will your heavenly Father? God doesn't leave His children empty-handed. He left you sealed by the Spirit, sustained by His strength, surrounded by His promises, and supplied with every spiritual blessing in heavenly places to help you succeed during your time here on earth (Matthew 16:19, Romans 8:17, Matthew 7:1, Ephesians 1:13, Ephesians 1:3).

When Jesus ascended, He didn't abandon us. He activated us. In John 14:3, He said that He was going away to prepare a place for us, but He also left Someone prepared in us. That's why the Holy Spirit didn't just fall on us; He now dwells in us. He's our divine deposit from above. He's Heaven's signature on our soul, saying, "This one belongs to me." This is because inheritance comes with identity, and that is...you are God's child!

The deeper you walk with the Father, the more access you unlock:

- if you know Him as provider, you will never panic or want for anything;
- if you know Him as healer, sickness can not shake you;
- if you know Him as deliverer, chains and shackles and forces trying to hinder your progress won't define you; and
- if you know Him as Father, you will stop begging like an orphan and claim your inheritance.

We don't just want His hand, we want to have the heart of God as well. Because the closer you draw to Him, the closer He draws to you, and the clearer you hear Him. And when you hear him, you stop falling for counterfeits. This is one of Satan's most strategic moves. He distracts us by getting us to focus on all the counterfeits under the guise of "You have to learn them, in order to avoid them." When really, all you have to do is learn the truth and all the other noise out there that comes our way will easily be detected as hype without substance, clouds without rain, and charisma without character—before they even enter your spiritual orbit and atmosphere.

That's why you walk like royalty, talk like royalty, operate like royalty: because you know what's yours, and more importantly, who you belong to.

But…let's be clear, the power isn't in the paperwork, it's in the proximity. There are many who know about God, but few who walk with Him. There are many who quote Scripture, but few who carry the signature of sonship. "Now if any man have not the Spirit of Christ, he is none of his" (Romans 8:9). That's not just theology, it's reality. The Spirit guides, guards, and governs the life of every heir. It's what keeps us standing when everything around us shakes. It's what helps us say no to the flesh and yes to the Father. It's what empowers us to live not just good lives, but godly ones.

And yet still, inheritance isn't just about receiving. It's about releasing what you have received. Because divine power isn't just for personal preservation, it's for public multiplication. You were not called just to survive. You were called to sow. You weren't anointed to hoard, you were anointed to harvest. This inheritance makes you a living epistle, mobile embassy, and a walking distribution center for divine glory.

The true sign of sonship is not just what you receive, it's what you reproduce. What good is inheritance if it ends with you? You've been blessed to be a blessing. You've been given power to pour it out. You've inherited Kingdom tools, and now it's time to do Kingdom work. Remember this: You are not a pauper. You are not a peasant. You are the King's kid. So abide, access, and advance, because what's in you is meant to change what's around you.

LAW 38

MULTIPLICATION IS THE MARK OF DIVINE POWER

"...Be fruitful and multiply..."

—GENESIS 1:28

The mission was never to maintain. It has always been to multiply.

The final phase of divine power isn't stillness—it's spread. The ultimate proof that Heaven touched Earth through your life isn't in how pretty you looked planted, but how many seeds sprang up after you. This law is not ornamental—it's agricultural. Multiplication is not an optional outcome—it's the expected evidence.

Jesus didn't just meet people. He moved people. He mobilized and multiplied. That's what divine power does—it advances the Kingdom.

When the woman at the well encountered Christ, she didn't leave with a business card—she left with a burden. She dropped her waterpot and picked up a mission. And what happened? "And many of the Samaritans of that city believed on him for the saying of the woman, which testified…" (John 4:39). That's multiplication. That's divine power made visible.

Fruitfulness has always been Heaven's litmus test for authenticity. From Genesis to Revelation, real power reproduces. God said to Adam, "…Be fruitful and multiply…" (Genesis 1:28). Jesus said, "…I have chosen you, and ordained you, that ye should go and bring forth fruit, and that your fruit should remain…" (John 15:16).

Even in judgment, the absence of fruit is the dividing line:

- The fig tree that Jesus cursed? It had leaves—but no fruit.
- The servant who buried his talent? Condemned not for what he did, but for what he didn't do.
- The branches not bearing fruit? Cut off.

Multiplication is not mere math. It is movement. It is mission. It is the Master's metric.

The world is full of artificial brilliance—high-definition charisma with zero divine residue. Social media influence. Platform pretense. Plastic pulpits. But nothing multiplies from it.

Why?

Because artificial things don't grow. They look like life—but have no seed. No struggle. No root. No seasons. Just decoration, not destiny.

That's why multiplication matters. It's how Heaven knows who's really His.

If Law 37 taught us that inheritance is released through intimacy, then Law 38 reveals what we're supposed to do with it: Advance. Advance the message. Advance the movement. Advance the mission.

If you have really walked in the fullness of divine power... If you have really healed from Law 27's Forgiveness... If you have truly rested in Law 35's Rhythm... If you have given Glory in Law 36 with all your might... Then you're ready to multiply.

Remember:

- The Church in Acts didn't just survive persecution; it multiplied because they were full of divine power.
- The loaves and fish—what was surrendered and blessed was multiplied.
- Abraham received a promise that his descendants would be as numerous as the stars. That promise didn't rest on his perfection, but on his faith and obedience—both of which are divine powers.

Divine power doesn't plateau. It progresses. It presses. It produces.

So, take inventory:

- Is what you're building bearing more than you?
- Is who you're becoming birthing faith in others?
- Have your scars multiplied healing in someone else?

If the answer is no—then stop playing it safe. Step into the soil. Drop the seed. Risk rejection. Risk ridicule. Risk reproduction.

Because you weren't filled to feel good—you were filled to fill others. You weren't anointed for applause—you were anointed for advancement. You weren't chosen to just chill— you were chosen to change lives.

LAW 39

MANTLES ARE FOR MOVEMENT

"...Elijah passed by him, and cast his mantle upon him. And he left the oxen, and ran after Elijah..."

—1 KINGS 19:19–20

Heaven doesn't hand out mantles for display in a museum. They are not ceremonial cloaks to be hung in glass cases or framed on walls of self-importance. They are not medals for memory's sake or decorative robes for the doubting. No—mantles are mandates. Mantles are mission. Mantles are movement.

A mantle is not just a garment—it is God's garment. It is symbolic of impartation, inheritance, and instruction. Elijah's mantle didn't just fall by accident. It descended by assignment.

When Elisha caught that mantle, he didn't sit still and simply savor the fabric. He struck the water and said, "...'Where is the LORD God of Elijah?'" (2 Kings 2:14). That's movement. That's mandate. That's multiplication. The parting of the Jordan River wasn't just a miracle—it was proof that Elisha had stepped into what he was anointed to do. But Elisha's story didn't stop there. After receiving Elijah's mantle, Elisha performed twice as many miracles as his predecessor: healing waters, multiplying oil, raising the dead, and opening the eyes of the blind. His ministry was marked by movement, momentum, and multiplication. He walked out the mantle until the mission was complete—until the day he died and, even then, the power of his mantle lingered. The bones of Elisha revived a man in his grave (2 Kings 13:21). That's legacy. That's movement beyond the man.

Too many in this generation are mantle collectors, not mantle carriers. They wear callings but refuse the cost. They quote verses but lack virtue. They want the platform but not the preparation. The mantle was never meant to be worn without movement. To wear it without walking is to waste the weight of Heaven's trust.

Let's make it plain:

Moses had a mantle—though his path was born in the bulrushes and raised in Pharaoh's palace, he moved in his mantle when he answered the burning bush. God's call was not to sit among royalty but to lead a rebellious people into freedom. Though timid at first, Moses moved with miracles, split the Red Sea, received the Law, and dwelt in God's presence so intimately that his face radiated glory. He didn't just wear the mantle; he walked it out until his final steps on Mount Nebo.

Joseph had a mantle—a coat of many colors that caused envy in his brothers but was a shadow of a greater mantle he would one day wear. Sold into slavery, lied about, locked in prison—yet Joseph moved in his God-ordained destiny. He interpreted dreams, managed famine, and ultimately saved Egypt and his own family. His mantle became a mission of mercy and provision, moving him from the pit to Pharaoh's palace.

David had a mantle—it wasn't King Saul's armor. That mantle was too big, too bulky, too human. When David tried on the king's armor to fight Goliath, it didn't fit. It was a symbol of human preparation, not divine power. So, he removed what man gave him and picked up what God blessed—five smooth stones and a sling. And with it, he dropped a giant and lifted a nation. The mantle of a shepherd boy became the throne of a king.

Jesus had a mantle—revealed at the Jordan River in full view of Heaven and Earth. As He came up from the waters, the heavens opened. The Father's voice declared, "…'This is my beloved Son, in whom I am well pleased'" (Matthew 3:17). The Holy Spirit descended like a dove. Father, Son, and Spirit in perfect unity—Power, Presence, and Purpose all converging on a single man. But immediately afterward, Jesus was led by the Spirit into the wilderness. Led—not left. Driven, but not deserted. And there, in the wilderness, the enemy tried to fracture the unity of the trinity.

In Matthew 4, Satan tells Jesus to bow to him; he was trying to usurp God's throne. Then, he asks Jesus to turn stones into bread, knowing Jesus was hungry and appealing to His vulnerability. Next, Satan takes Jesus to the highest point of the temple and says Jesus should throw Himself down. He was attempting to manipulate the mantle by tempting God's promises. But Jesus, in every temptation, responded with the Word. The mantle didn't wither in weakness—it withstood it. The mission moved forward. From there, Jesus launched into a ministry that turned the world upside down, not with might, but with mercy. Not with armies, but with authority. His was a mantle of miracles, mercy, and the message of eternal life. And He wore it all the way to the cross.

Mantles come with movement because divine power was

never designed for stagnation. The anointing flows—not freezes. Purpose pulls you forward. Calling commands you to come. And Heaven is watching to see—are you wearing it or wasting it?

You may say, "But I don't feel qualified." Neither did Jeremiah. Neither did Gideon. Neither did Mary, the mother of Jesus. But when God places the mantle on your life, He places His might in your spirit. "…Not by might, nor by power, but by my spirit, saith the Lord of Hosts" (Zechariah 4:6).

The mantle doesn't always mean you're ready. It means you're responsible.

So, pick up that dream again. Move in that calling again. Preach with fire. Parent with purpose. Serve with strength. Create with courage. Build with boldness. You're not just covered—you're called. And that call requires a move.

Because mantles left idle will mildew. But mantles in motion multiply.

Don't die draped in destiny you never deployed. Don't spend your life admiring a calling you never activated. Heaven's hand is on your life, and it's time to walk like it. Time to war like it. Time to work like it.

If you've got the mantle, you've got the movement. So move.

LAW 40

AUTHORITY REQUIRES ACCOUNTABILITY

"So then every one of us shall give account of himself to God."
—ROMANS 14:12

If you carry divine weight, you must walk with divine responsibility.

Power isn't just a possession. It is a stewardship, a sacred trust. Authority is not a toy for the immature or a trophy for the insecure. It is a divine delegation of God's own Spirit, and the Holy Spirit is not a genie to be manipulated nor a force to be faked. He is God, and to treat Him as common is to court catastrophe.

The early church knew this truth in real time.

In Acts 5 we meet Ananias and Sapphira, a couple who wanted the applause of the faithful without the authority of faithfulness. They sold land but withheld part of the proceeds, pretending that they had given it all to the Church. Their sin wasn't just in the math; it was in the motive. Peter, being full of the Holy Spirit, confronted them with a thunderous rebuke: "…thou hast not lied unto men, but unto God" (5:4). And the couple dropped dead where they stood. Not because God was petty, but because He is pure. His church was just being established, and the pattern and standards had to be clear. The Holy Spirit is not to be lied on, lied to, or leveraged for social gain. Divine power comes with divine consequences.

Paul echoed this truth to the Ephesians: "…and grieve not the holy Spirit of God, whereby ye are sealed unto the day of redemption" (v. 4:30). Grieving the Spirit is not about offending a fragile deity, it's about violating an intimate relationship. The Holy Spirit is our seal, our sustainer, and our source, and when we walk in arrogance, bitterness, deceit, manipulation, or moral compromise, we invite grief to the very one who gives us grace.

We want the anointing but forget that the anointing is costly. Oil comes from crushing. And when the oil flows, so must reverence. It's not about "I got the gift," it's about "Does the gift still have me?"

In Acts chapter 19, we find a group of Jewish exorcists who decided to use Jesus's name like a spell to exorcise some demons: We adjure you by the Jesus whom Paul preaches…but the demons responded, "Paul I know, but who are you?" And they beat that man like he stole something. Actually, he did. He tried to steal the power and authority of Christ that was not his to have, and the Bible says they beat him until he was bloody and naked. They didn't beat the brakes off of him, but they definitely beat his clothes off of him.

You see, they had no relationship with Jesus—none. They had no covering. They had no accountability. They tried to invoke what they had not been entrusted with. That's spiritual identity theft, and it will get you evicted in battles you're not licensed to enter.

Then there is King Uzziah. He began his reign with humility, seeking God and prospering. But his pride swelled with his power. He entered the temple to burn incense, a role reserved only for priests. God struck him with leprosy, and he lived out the rest of his days isolated. His kingship was tainted by dishonor. Why? Because spiritual roles carry sacred restrictions. You can not bypass accountability and expect to hold onto authority. In short, he failed to stay in his lane.

My brothers and sisters, we are not owners of the Holy Spirit. We are temples. We house His presence, but He owns the title deed to His place of residence. To wield power without being under God's hand is to court spiritual bankruptcy.

That authority that casts out demons, heals the sick, speaks with wisdom, and preaches with power must be continually checked at the altar of accountability.

If you preach under power but harbor pride… If you prophesy but manipulate people emotionally… If you lay hands but refuse to live holy… Then the authority you walk in becomes an illusion, and you risk forfeiting the grace that gave it to you.

Divine power doesn't make you untouchable. It makes you more accountable. And this is grace. Because what God gives, He guards. He disciplines those He loves. He corrects those He crowns. So let this law ring like thunder and burn like fire:

- If you will walk in His name, you must bow to His nature.
- If you speak for Him, you must live for Him.
- If you carry His authority, you must answer to His accountability.

Will you be faithful over what you've been given? Will you pass the test of authority by honoring the accountability that comes with it? Because in the Kingdom, misuse can lead to disuse, but humility leads to overflow. So, let's go deeper. Let's go higher. Let's walk worthy of the power we've been entrusted with.

LAW 41

STEWARDSHIP SUSTAINS SUPPLY

"Moreover it is required in stewards, that a man be found faithful."
—I CORINTHIANS 4:2

Stewardship is the soil in which a sustained supply will take root.

This is not a vending machine gospel. God is not a cosmic genie that responds to our declarations like incantations. This is not name it and claim it. This is carry it and cultivate it. Divine power is not a shortcut for spiritual responsibility; it is the result of it. How we manage what we've been given reveals whether we're ready to carry more.

You might be asking yourself, "So, what is stewardship?" Well, here is your answer. Stewardship is the divine discipline of managing what you've been entrusted with as though it belongs to the King—because, in actuality, it does. It is the understanding that every breath, every dollar, every opportunity, every relationship, and every gift is on loan from Heaven, and how you handle it either qualifies you or disqualifies you for more. You see, the oil never continues to flow where the vessel continues to leak. The blessings of God are not wasted on wasteful hands.

Allow me to elaborate on the issues of mismanagement and misalignment. In Matthew 25, Jesus tells us a story that stings the spirit if you truly listen. It goes like this: A master gives his servants talents, five, two, and one—"...to every man according to his several ability..." (25:15). The five- and two-talent servants doubled what they were given. But the one-talent servant buried his, blaming fear and the character of the master as his excuse.

The master's rebuke of his excuse was swift and scorching: "...Thou wicked and slothful servant... Thou oughtest therefore to have put my money to the exchangers... Take therefore the talent from him, and give it unto him which hath ten talents" (25:26–28).

Laziness is not just weakness, it's wickedness when it comes to the things of God. Burying your gift, your time, your purpose, your power...is rebellion wrapped in passivity.

Stewardship is the proof of divine partnership. And when you fail to partner with Heaven, you forfeit Heaven's provision.

Let's look at another story where stewarding went well.

Joseph didn't just manage grain in Egypt. He managed pain in prison, promotion in Potiphar's house, and power in Pharaoh's palace. In every phase, he stewarded well. His stewardship not only sustained the supply of food during a famine but also the future of Israel. When God saw how he handled confinement, He knew he could handle command. The question isn't: can you shout in church? The question is: can you still serve in obscurity? Can you be trusted with a little before you're entrusted with a lot? Because stewardship is not seasonal. It's character that carries across chapters.

Sustained supply is not a reward, but a result. Let's dismantle the deception. God is not manipulated by noise. He is moved by obedience. You can't sow irresponsibility and reap outpouring.

If you want sustained provision, sustained influence, sustained divine presence, then check the stewardship of your:

- Time—Are you managing your minutes or misplacing them?
- Gifts—Are you sharpening them or shelving them?
- Relationships—Are you nourishing them or neglecting them?
- Resources—Are you budgeting them or bleeding them?

Supply does not flow into chaos. It flows through order and obedience.

Somewhere along the way, we have become an entitled generation and now have confused inheritance with entitlement, but there is a difference.

Inheritance is given, but it must be stewarded to multiply. Entitlement demands, but often destroys what it receives.

You don't demand power. You demonstrate maturity. You don't claim increase. You cultivate what you already have. God responds to faithfulness formulas.

Are you ready to be whole, feel whole? Then, let's go deeper into the fullness of divine power. Let's not waste what we've been given; let's multiply it. Let's steward with excellence, and trust God to supply with abundance. Because what you steward will determine what God will understand.

LAW 42

WHOLENESS PRECEDES WITNESS

"... Go home to thy friends, and tell them how great things the Lord hath done for thee, and hath had compassion on thee."

—MARK 5:19

You don't just represent Him with your words, you reveal Him with your wholeness.

Before your mouth opens to preach, your life has already spoken.

Before your hands reach out to heal, your heart must first be made whole.

Before you wear His name in the streets, you must welcome His love in your secret place.

This is not about perfection, but completion. Not flawlessness, but fullness. Not being without blemish, but being without broken allegiance. The true witness of divine power is not how loud you declare, but how whole you walk.

Many have looked at believers, and the church at large, calling her "The Sleeping Giant," as she has yet to reach her full potential and divine power. "Awake though that sleepest, and arise from the dead, and Christ shall give thee light." Ephesians 5:14 suggested this thousands of years ago, and yet, we are still sleeping. We have tried and failed to improve on the mandate, which is really quite simple: "And ye are complete in him, which is the head of all principality and power" (Colossians 2:10).

You are not complete in your resume.

You are not complete in your relationships.

You are not complete in your bank account, your brand, or your brilliance.

You are complete in Him, Christ, the cornerstone of your confidence. And until you are rooted in that reality, your witness will always wobble. Wholeness is not the absence of wounds. It's the presence of healing. It is the soul-sure belief that you are loved, not for what you do, but because of whose you are. Believe that, and never doubt it.

"There is no fear in love; but perfect love casteth out fear..." (1 John 4:18). Fear will fracture your faith. Doubt will dilute your dominion. And both will hijack your witness.

You can not evangelize effectively if you're still wondering whether God really loves you. But when you let His perfect love perfect you, when you accept that you are fully known yet fully loved, when you recognize that His grace is your glue, your guide, and your guard, then suddenly, the power of divine love becomes the fuel of divine witness.

Fear flees. Shame evaporates. And the soul finds rest in righteousness.

Let's look at a biblical pattern of witness before and after wholeness.

There was a woman who went to the well to draw water.

She was one with five failed relationships—broken, weary, and rejected. Yet one encounter with Jesus, and she becomes a living well for her city.

Why?

Because Jesus didn't just give her a mic, He gave her wholeness. He didn't just say, "Go witness." He gave her worth. And worth precedes witness. She dropped her water jar, ran back into the city, and said, "'Come, see a man, which told me all things that ever I did…" (John 4:29).

She didn't quote the Torah.

She didn't heal the sick.

She simply became whole, and her wholeness drew the crowd, and many believed as a result of her words.

You see, a broken witness may win crowds, but lose credibility. They may gather attention, but scatter anointing. Because your wounds, when left unhealed, leak poison instead of power, leak infection instead of influence.

That's why wholeness is not optional, it's foundational to fullness.

- A father wounds a family if he hasn't first addressed his own.
- A leader limps through decisions if they're still bleeding from betrayal.
- A prophet can't see clearly if they're still peering through the prism of personal pain.

Wholeness makes your witness weighty. Perhaps you want to manifest this divine power and want to apply wholeness to your life; if that is the case, then do this:

1. Receive His love daily—Not based on performance, but position. You are a son/daughter. That means you are loved without loopholes.
2. Renew Your Mind Continuously—Your identity must be rehearsed until it becomes revelation.
3. Release What Healed You—Don't hoard the help. Your healing is someone else's hope. You don't have to be perfect, but just whole enough to say, "I've been there and God brought me through."

When you are whole, you radiate wholeness.

Wholeness walks into a room before you say a word. It draws those who are seeking, searching, starving for something real.

You become the epistle. You become the testimony. You become the evidence of power. And power isn't always loud. Sometimes it's simply whole.

Wholeness is not a destination, it's a divine decision to rest in His love, to walk in His truth, and to witness from your healing, not your hurting.

You are complete in Him. You are called by Him. And your wholeness…is your supernatural signal to the world.

LAW 43

WITNESS IS A WEAPON

> *"And they overcame him by the blood of the Lamb, and by the word of their testimony; and they loved not their lives unto the death…"*
> —REVELATION 12:11

Your voice isn't just a vessel—it's a weapon forged in the fire of divine encounters.

You are evidence.

Your scars preach louder than sermons. Your survival is a scroll. Your story is a sword. When the enemy comes in like a flood, the power of your witness lifts a standard. You may not have walked the dusty roads of Galilee, but your witness still walks tall in the courtroom of darkness. You may not have touched the hem of His garment, but you've been touched. And what He touched, He transformed—and what He transformed, He now trusts to testify.

This is not passive piety. This is spiritual warfare through sacred storytelling. This is rescue in real-time, where demons tremble when the redeemed speak boldly of their Deliverer.

Because the moment you open your mouth and recount what God has done, you set off a divine detonation. Heaven applauds. Hell recoils. Chains rattle loose. Witnessing is warfare, and your words are weapons.

When Jesus left the ninety-nine to pursue the one, it wasn't divine disregard—it was divine demonstration. He wanted the ninety-nine to understand the weight of one soul. That's the essence of witness. It's not about boasting in ourselves but broadcasting the love of the Savior who found us when we were forgotten, forgave us when we were filthy, and freed us when we were finished.

That one wandering sheep? That was you. That was me. Our witness is not a weapon of pride but of piercing love—a reminder that the One who found us will never fail to find the next.

Hebrews 12:1 begins by stating, "Wherefore seeing we also are compassed about with so great a cloud of witnesses..." These aren't casual bystanders. These are the battle-scarred saints who finished their race, who stood the test, who triumphed by trust. They are cheering from the balcony of eternity—Moses with his staff, David with his sling, Esther with her courage, Paul with his pen, and your grandmother with her prayers. Their stories are your strength. Their survival is your signal. And their witness reminds you: Don't quit now. God is faithful. You're closer than you think.

This world doesn't need more polished speeches—it needs raw, redemptive testimonies. The kind that says, "I was addicted, but now I'm anointed. I was lost, but now I lead. I was bitter, but now I bless."

That's your power. That's your purpose. That's your weapon.

And don't get it twisted—this is urgency with eternity in mind. The clock of grace is ticking. The era of Gentile harvest is approaching its crescendo. Satan knows his time is short, which is why he's attacking your story, your self-worth, and your memory. Because if he can silence your witness, he can stifle your warfare. But God has not called you to be silent. God has not equipped you with divine power solely for your own private peace. You've been empowered to proclaim.

When Paul and Silas were locked in prison, they didn't just pray—they praised. And when they praised, the prison shook. Why? Because praise is a form of witness. It's the declaration that God is still good, even when the cell is still closed. And when that kind of witness is unleashed, freedom flows, not just for you—but for those listening.

Your life is not light because you hide it. Your life is light because you shine it.

Witnessing is not just what you say—it's how you live.

How you love.

How you stand.

How you suffer.

How you forgive.

You are the walking proof of power. The living evidence of God's mercy. The breathing billboard of divine grace.

This Law is a call to arms and a call to altar. Your witness is not just a memory—it's a ministry. You are carrying Heaven's message in an earthly vessel. Your past has been repurposed, your pain has been anointed, and your voice has been verified by your victory.

So, tell it. Speak it. Proclaim it. Post it. Preach it. Share it. Shout it. Live it.

Because every time you do, you drive a dagger into darkness and launch light into a lost world.

Because true divine power isn't proven in what you gain—

It's in what you give.

What you leave.
What you impart.
And what will still speak, long after you are silent.

LAW 44

LEGACY IS GREATER THAN LOYALTY TO SELF

"A good man leaveth an inheritance to his children's children…"
—PROVERBS 13:22

What will they say about you when you're gone?

Will it be the car you drove or the Christ you carried?

Will it be the size of your bank account or the strength of your belief?

Will it be your assets…or your anointing?

Legacy is not about longevity—it's about leaving.

Leaving something behind. Leaving someone better.

Not merely leaving money, but making meaning.

Not just passing along riches, but planting roots of righteousness.

And while you won't find the English word "legacy" in the

scriptures, you'll find its fingerprints on every page—etched in stone tablets, woven into family lines, passed through covenants, and cut into callings. Legacy isn't about labeling something "yours." It's about launching something greater than yourself.

Let's begin in the world of men before we rise into the realm of the Spirit. In everyday terms, legacy is what you hand down from one generation to the next. It's the residue of your reputation. It's the echo of your decisions, values, and vision. Legacy is not just inheritance—it is intention. It is investment. It is intergenerational stewardship.

But even the best of earthly legacies fade. Money devalues. Properties crumble. Businesses collapse. But a godly name? Now that endures.

"A good name is rather to be chosen than great riches, and loving favour rather than silver and gold" (Proverbs 22:1).

This verse bridges us beautifully to a higher plane. A name is not just a label—it is a life story. It is the substance of your soul engraved in syllables. To have a good name is to have lived with integrity, consistency, and courage. And to leave behind loving favor—that's legacy in full bloom. That's divine favor passed down as a fragrant memory and a spiritual inheritance.

Hebrews 11 gives us our hall of faith—not hall of fame. These were not flawless men and women, but faithful ones. Abel offered a more excellent sacrifice, "and by it he being dead yet speaketh" (v. 4). That's legacy. Noah built when others mocked. Abraham walked when others stayed. Sarah believed when others doubted. Rahab hid the spies and rerouted the plan of God.

They left behind no bank accounts. But they left behind belief accounts that still draw spiritual interest today.

And what about Paul? He told young Timothy that his sincere faith lived first in his grandmother Lois and mother Eunice. Faith passed on: not fortune, not fame, but faith.

Now lift your eyes higher—what of our Savior?

Jesus did not die to be remembered. He died so that we might live.

In John 17 we hear the Son speaking to the Father—not in whispers of defeat, but in declarations of destiny: "I have given them thy word... As thou hast sent me into the world, even so have I also sent them into the world" (17:14,18). This is no ordinary prayer. It is the capstone of His mission, the signature on His legacy. Jesus does not ask for Himself; He intercedes for His disciples—and for all who would believe through their word. He prays that we might be kept in His name, sanctified in His truth, and unified in His love. In this prayer He hands over more than memories—He hands over His mission. He seals His legacy not with ink, but with intercession.

And what a legacy it is. He denied Himself and gave us Himself. He left behind not palaces or possessions, but the very presence of the Holy Spirit. He bequeathed to us the cross as our covering, the church as our community, and everlasting life as our crown. His prayer stretches across centuries, reaching into our generation, binding us to the blessing of being His. Here we see legacy in its purest form: not loyalty to self, but loyalty to the will of the Father and to the good of others. By this prayer, Christ extended His legacy into every life that would ever believe, proving that true legacy is not what you hold onto—it is what you hand down.

Will your grandchildren remember your prayers or just your purchases?

Will your coworkers remember your excellence or your ego?

Will your friends recall your generosity or your grind?

Legacy is what lives when you leave.

Your choices. Your courage. Your compassion.

Did you pass on wisdom? Or just wealth?

Did you cultivate character? Or just comfort?

When your name is spoken at your funeral, will it fall like a feather—or thunder like a charge?

To be loyal to self is to live small. To protect your corner. Build your empire. "Store up treasures…where moth and rust destroy…" (Matthew 6:19 AMP).

But to live for legacy is to live large. To give generously. To mentor fiercely. To invest your days like seed, not spend them like coins. It is to die empty, knowing you left everything on the field and in the hearts of those who needed it most.

That's divine power—reproduced, replicated, released.

It doesn't terminate in you. It travels through you.

This is the fullness section of the book, and legacy is not a final destination—it's a divine transfer station.

It says, "What God gave me, I didn't hoard. I handed it down."

It says, "What I was taught, I taught. What I endured, I used. What I saw, I shared."

And in this, legacy becomes a ministry.

You don't need a pulpit. You need a purpose.

You don't need a title. You need a testimony.

You don't need applause. You need a heart that cares more about what echoes after you than what exalts you now.

LAW 45

POWER FLOWS TO THE POURED OUT

"For I am now ready to be offered, and the time of my departure is at hand…"

—2 TIMOTHY 4:6

Power, by divine design, flows.

It doesn't sit. It doesn't stagnate.

It flows like a river. It pours like oil. It moves like wind.

It transforms, it transfers, and—through the surrendered—it transcends.

This is not just poetry. It is principle.

It's not merely metaphor. It's mechanics—both heavenly and physical.

Let us now enter the realm of spirit and science, and see how God's glory flows through the vessel who refuses to hoard Heaven's help.

"In the last days, saith God, I will pour out of my Spirit upon all flesh..." (Acts 2:17, quoting Joel 2:28). He didn't sprinkle. He didn't mist. He poured.

From the prophetic foreshadowing in Joel to the very first outpouring in Acts, the release of divine power was never a casual flicker—it was a forceful flow. And when He pours, He empowers.

The Spirit is not just a sign of divine presence—it is the power line of divine performance. The Spirit came like a rushing mighty wind, yet He also speaks in a still small voice. He's not bound by form, but always governed by function. He moves according to assignment. He fills according to surrender. He flows where there's room.

In electrical engineering, power is not just stored—it is converted and transferred.

The faster the energy flows, the more powerful the system.

And that is what Heaven looks for: conductors, not containers.

The capacitor stores, but the conductor flows.

The resistor blocks, but the current moves.

What are you in the Kingdom?

A hoarder of blessings or a conduit of breakthrough?

Do you worship to consume, or to channel?

Do you pray for performance, or to become a platform for God's glory?

In divine physics, the more you pour, the more He flows.

You were never meant to be a reservoir. You were meant to be a river.

Jesus said, "'But you shall receive power after that the Holy Ghost is come upon you...'" (Acts 1:8). Then He said, "...and greater works than these shall he do; because I go unto my father..." (John 14:12).

How can we do greater works than the Son of God? Because

the Spirit multiplies. It doesn't just descend—it distributes. And where it finds a vessel willing to pour, it performs.

This is divine force multiplication. The Spirit doesn't just flow to fill you—it flows through you to touch others. Your song lifts others. Your gift unlocks others. Your prayer covers others.

Your witness wins others. You are a force multiplier!

And the more you pour, the more power is produced. That's spiritual conductivity.

Paul caught this revelation when he wrote: "For I am now ready to be offered, and the time of my departure is at hand…" (2 Timothy 4:6). He knew he wasn't meant to preserve himself. He was meant to present himself.

He didn't die full—he died empty.

And his power reached further because he poured deeper.

Your greatest impact will come not from what you protect, but from what you release.

Our Savior poured until He had nothing left but a borrowed tomb.

He poured His time. He poured His tears. He poured His life.

He poured Himself into twelve broken men, who then turned the world upside down.

And even as He ascended, He sent us the Spirit—not to be hidden, but to be heralded.

His pouring became our power.

In physics, resistance reduces flow.

So it is in the Spirit. Bitterness is a resistor. Fear is a resistor. Pride, shame, greed—each one dampens the current.

But when you strip it all away, when you become vulnerable, surrendered, and obedient—your life becomes a live wire of divine voltage. You begin to spark revival just by being present. You begin to shift rooms just by walking in. You begin to move atmospheres just by opening your mouth.

You are now functioning as you were designed to—flowing.

To dam the river is to rob the land of its natural flow. To hoard divine power is to halt Heaven's reach. But when you pour, God provides more. When you give, He gives again.

That's the law of divine flow. That's the rhythm of the river. That's how power flows to the poured out.

The world doesn't need more containers. It needs conduits. It needs people who pour. People who refuse to be bottlenecks in the bloodstream of Heaven.

Pour your praise.

Pour your time.

Pour your wisdom.

Pour your prayers.

Pour your love.

And when you do, watch the heavens open.

LAW 46

THE POWER OF LOVE

"Let all your things be done with charity."
—1 CORINTHIANS 16:14

They sang it in the '80s—"I Want to Know What Love Is."
They searched for it in Shakespeare.
They wept for it in sonnets.
They bled for it in battlefields.
They fantasized about it in fairy tales.
But few have ever fully found it, and fewer still have faithfully lived it.
That's because what most call love…is lust. What many celebrate as love…is sentiment. What often starts with butterflies ends with betrayal.
Why?
Because true love isn't anchored in feelings—it is founded in faithfulness.
The layers of love: Eros, Philia, and Agape. Let us exegete (explain) the layers of love as scripture does:

Eros is the sensual, emotional love. Good. God-ordained. But seasonal. It warms the bed, but it cannot weather the storm.

Philia is the loyal, brotherly love. Needed. Noble. But it's reciprocal. It stands with you when you're lovable, but may shrink when you're low.

But Agape…

Agape is the divine distinction. The relentless, redeeming, resilient love.

The unreasonable love.

The undeserved love.

The kind that chooses you when everything else walks away.

It doesn't quit. It doesn't count. It doesn't keep receipts. Agape says:

"You messed up. I'll still stand up."

"You ran off. I'll run after."

"You failed. I'm still faithful."

We've heard 1 Corinthians 13 read at weddings, and seen it printed on pillows and framed in foyers.

Love is patient. Love is kind. It does not envy, it does not boast…

But let's be clear. This passage isn't a checklist for your spouse. It's not ammunition for your arguments. It's not your license to leave when they no longer meet the measurement.

No, beloved…

This is a portrait of the Person of Christ.

This is how Jesus loves you.

This is His patience when you pout.

This is His kindness when you're careless.

This is His mercy when you misstep.

This thirteenth chapter was never meant to be a magnifying glass to judge others.

It was meant to be a mirror to reflect Christ.

"Love keeps no receipts of wrongs."
He erased the ledger.
"Love always wins!"
He stayed when we strayed.

When we understand this—really grasp it—not only do we fall deeper in love with God, we stop holding the people around us hostage to a standard we ourselves cannot sustain.

Real love is a decision, not a dopamine rush.

Too many think love is found when it must be formed.

They chase feelings, but feelings are fickle.

They crave chemistry, but real love requires covenant.

Love, true love, is a choice in the face of change,

A commitment in the face of crisis,

A sacrifice in the face of selfishness.

And until we learn that love is decisive, we'll keep getting derailed by disappointment.

When you see love as Christ sees it, it doesn't just change how you treat your spouse...

It changes how you:

- Respond to that indifferent boss who ignores your value.
- Endure that jealous coworker who mimics your excellence but despises your light.
- Forgive that hateful relative who hurt you and hasn't healed themselves.

Real love—the divine kind—isn't reserved for romance.

It is revealed in restraint.

It is shown in serving.

It is proven in pain.

This is the power of love—not just to feel, but to forbear.

To love like God loves you—not based on worth, but based on His will.

"Greater love hath no man than this: that a man lay down his life for his friends" (John 15:13).

He laid it down so we could rise up.

He was wounded so we could be washed.

He was pierced so we could be powered.

And when you love like this, hell has no answer. This is the divine weapon. The final frontier. The blazing, beating heart of God's power.

Let the love of Christ transform you.

Let it tame you.

Let it teach you how to love beyond the wound, beyond the betrayal, beyond the breakup, beyond the blow.

Fall in love with the One who first loved you.

And from that place of unshakeable, irrevocable, indestructible love—

You'll begin to pour out what He has poured in.

LAW 47

GLORY WITHOUT GOD IS GRAVEYARD DUST

"Except the LORD build the house, they labour in vain that build it…"

—PSALM 127:1

Glory.

Everybody wants it.

Rappers rap about it.

Athletes chase it.

Preachers—some—pimp it.

But very few understand it, and even fewer are willing to return it to the rightful One.

Glory is not a spotlight.

It's a weight.

Not a trophy—but a test.

And when we keep what only God is supposed to get—we sign a contract with decay.

This is what I mean when I say:

Glory without God is graveyard dust.

Let history and Scripture testify. "Thine, O Lord, is the greatness, and the power, and the glory, and the victory, and the majesty..." (1 Chronicles 29:11). Not ours, but His.

Lucifer—the luminous one, the anointed cherub—desired glory. Not just to bask in it... but to own it.

"I will ascend...I will exalt...I will sit..." (Isaiah 14:13).

But all that "I" made him fall.

And so it is with all those who try to cosign God's credit. They ultimately end up bankrupt.

Nebuchadnezzar built Babylon, and he believed it was his brilliance that bore the blueprint. He looked over his kingdom and declared, "Look at what I have built!" God humbled him—made him eat grass like an ox.

Why? Because glory is God's alone.

Herod, adored by the people, gave a speech so eloquent that they called him a god. But because he did not give glory to God, he was struck down and eaten by worms.

Friend, glory is not a garment to wear—it's a mirror to reflect. And when you hoard it, Heaven halts your harvest.

But now, let's flip it—

Let's behold the beauty and battle power of giving God glory.

At Jericho, the walls didn't fall because of swords or siege towers...

Josuha 6:16 tells us they fell because of shouts of praise and obedient worship. "Shout, for the Lord has given you the city!" It wasn't a cry of complaint—it was a cry of glory. And the earth responded.

In 2 Chronicles 20 (KJV), when Jehoshaphat and his crew were outnumbered and outmuscled, they didn't call for more weapons—they called for worshippers.

"...'Praise the Lord, for His mercy endures forever!'" And what happened? The enemy's armies turned on each other. Worship confused the wicked.

At midnight, Paul and Silas didn't moan, groan, or sulk. They sang. And glory cracked the chains. Praise pried open prison doors.

The power of glory doesn't stop in the past—it permeates eternity. "...the whole earth is full of his glory..." (Isaiah 6:3). "And the city had no need of the sun, neither of the moon, to shine in it: for the glory of God did lighten it..." (Revelation 21:23). Glory is Heaven's electricity.

It is the current of God's Kingdom. It is the light that radiates from the throne—unfiltered, unending, undiluted.

And here's the scandal of grace:

God allows us—a broken, bruised, born-again people—to carry that glory. But we must never confuse carrying it with claiming it. We are the lamps—He is the light. We are the instrument—He is the inspiration. We are the echo—He is the voice.

So, if you build your platform on self-glory, you will be buried beneath it. If you take the credit, prepare to pay the cost. If you try to be the glory, you will end up buried in graveyard dust.

But if you give it back... If you redirect every compliment... If you deflect every spotlight... If you bow before you boast... Then glory becomes your covering, not your coffin.

LAW 48

FULLNESS IS FOUND IN FINISHING WELL

"I have fought a good fight, I have finished my course, I have kept the faith."

—2 TIMOTHY 4:7

They tried to break you.

They betrayed you.

You've been bruised, belittled, and burdened.

You've walked through fire with no applause.

You've fought silent battles.

You've smiled through storms.

You've cried in corners where no one knew your name.

Yet here you are—still standing. That's not weakness. That's divine power on display.

That's what this final law is all about: not how you started, not what you lost, not even what you dreamed…but how you finish.

Fullness doesn't come without fire.

Purpose doesn't arrive without pain.

If you've lived long enough, you've been misunderstood, mistreated, maybe even misused.

But what if I told you that every betrayal had a blueprint?

What if the breaking was really a birthing? What if each wound was a workout?

And what if every loss was a divine classroom…where God whispered, "I'm building you for something greater."

Joseph was sold into slavery—but he finished in the palace.

Ruth buried her husband—but she finished in Boaz's field.

Jesus was pierced and spit on—but He finished with all power in His hands.

Friend, divine power doesn't prevent the pit—it redeems it. It doesn't always cancel the crisis—it converts it. And now, the question isn't what happened to you.

The question is:

What will happen through you?

And now we arrive at this final law, standing at the summit with sacred clarity:

Fullness is found in finishing well.

Forget Maslow. There is a mountain higher than self-actualization. Let us ascend a new peak—a pyramid reconstructed by revelation:

- At the base? Surrender: acknowledging that you are not the source.
- Then comes identity: understanding you are a child of God.
- Then connection: abiding in intimacy, walking with the Spirit.
- Then function: using gifts, stewarding power, impacting others.

- Then multiplication: producing fruit, discipling, pouring out.
- Then glory: not for you, but returned to God.

And at the pinnacle?

Fullness. Completion. All of Him, and none of me. That is the real peak. Not a platform. Not applause. Not accolades.

But to say, like Paul: "I have finished my course." Or like Jesus: "It is finished."

That, my friend, is divine power in full bloom.

Now I speak directly to you—yes, you—the one holding this book:

You were born with potential.

But potential is just a promise until it's finished.

You've been given gifts. But gifts unopened gather dust.

You've endured pain. But pain unused becomes poison.

So now the question isn't: do you have power?

The question is: what will you do with it?

The Holy Spirit is in you. The Father loves you. Jesus paid it all.

And now you stand at the edge of divine deployment.

So, I leave you with this:

Run your race.

Pour out your oil.

Empty your alabaster jar.

Finish your assignment.

Leave nothing on the table.

And when the time comes, die empty—so Heaven can say, "Well done."

Because fullness is not found in doing everything…it's found in finishing the one thing God called you to do.

PART III SUMMARY

From Foundation…to Function…to Fullness
   Let us not forget the journey:
   You've walked the path from foundation to function.
   You learned that divine power starts with surrender.
   You declared weakness as the womb of wisdom.
   You anchored in the Holy Spirit, not in hustle.
   You saw that God's yes doesn't need man's applause.
   You moved with momentum.
   You discovered joy is our stabilizer, excellence our expansion, compassion our currency.
   You learned miracles move through movement, that serving unlocks supernatural strategy, and that timing trumps talent.
   You were reminded that giving God glory is not optional—it's oxygen.
   And now you have stood in the brilliance of fullness.
   Here, the light grew brighter.
   Here, the lessons were not just principles to learn but postures to live. You've seen that divine power is not a moment—it

is a movement. Not a tool—it is a trust. Not a trophy to display—but a treasure to steward.

In this final stretch, you have embraced that Heaven's power is not given for personal gain but for Kingdom glory. You have learned that authority demands accountability, that legacy must outlive loyalty to self, and that love is the highest force in the universe. You have discovered that to be poured out is not to be emptied but to be filled again with the overflow of God's Spirit.

This is the fullness: to walk so deeply in God's presence that your life itself becomes a witness; to move under His mantle without hesitation; to leave a trail of blessing that extends beyond your years; to let every breath, every step, every word echo Heaven's heart.

The fullness of divine power is not the end of the journey—it is the beginning of the assignment.

You are not merely a recipient of this power; you are now a carrier of it. Go forth in the strength of the Lord, knowing that the One who called you is faithful to complete the work He began in you.

This is fullness. This is stewardship. This…is divine power in motion.

CONCLUSION

The Divine Power in You

You made it. You didn't just read a book—you scaled a mountain.

From the Foundation of divine identity to the Function of supernatural action, all the way into the Fullness of Christ-centered completion—you have walked through fire and revelation, law by law, line by line, precept upon precept.

And now, standing at the summit of it all, I ask you:

What will you do with this power?

You've been poured into. Now it's your turn to pour out. You've been equipped. Now it's your moment to engage. You've been informed. Now, rise and be transformed.

Not for likes. Not for applause. Not for clout. But for the Kingdom, for the calling, for Christ.

Because if divine power doesn't move you, doesn't mature you, doesn't mobilize you, then it hasn't met you yet.

You were not built to live a lukewarm, low-impact, half-hearted life. You were made to set the captives free, speak truth in trembling rooms, heal broken systems, and walk in uncommon wisdom.

You are not a whisper. You are a windstorm of worship wrapped in human skin. And the world is waiting on you to wake up.

This power was never about personal platform. It was never just about you at all. It was always about divine positioning.

Not about your rise, but about His reign. Not about spotlight, but about stewardship. Not about influence, but about intercession. Not about gaining ground, but about glorifying God.

You now walk in something the world cannot cancel, culture cannot comprehend, and hell cannot handle.

And don't forget: The anointing doesn't need announcement. The oil speaks for itself. Let your witness be your weapon. Let your scars be your sermon.

What the world needs now is not more intellectual debates, not more churchy clichés, not more artificial influencers.

It needs real ones. Real light in dark places. Real people with real power. People like you—who've been through real storms, real scars, real soul-stretching seasons, and still stand with faith, fire, and forgiveness.

You don't need another motivational speech. You need a moment like this, where something clicks inside, where the veil tears just a little more, where you hear Heaven whisper:

Now, go! You're ready!

The divine pyramid of power has now been revealed. And at the top? It isn't self-actualization. It's soul-surrender.

You are not climbing for greatness. You are being called into God's greatness.

There is still a giant sleeping in the Church, still a generation unsure of its divine authority, still a remnant that doesn't realize they've been endued with power from on high.

But that's about to change. Because you are the remnant. And this book—these forty-eight laws—were your activation.

If you ever feel weak again, remember Law 1: Divine Power Begins in Weakness. If your motives grow muddy, return to Law 36: Give Glory or Lose Grace. And if you ever feel empty, finish again at Law 48: Fullness Is Found in Finishing Well.

This is the journey of divine power. Not a sprint. Not a show. Not a game. But a sacred mission from Heaven to Earth, where ordinary vessels carry extraordinary glory.

And as long as there's breath in your body, there is divine power flowing through your bones.

Walk like you've been chosen. Pray like you've been empowered. Serve like Heaven is watching. Preach without platform. Worship without worry. And finish your race with fire in your belly and grace in your grip.

You've read *The 48 Laws of Divine Power*.

You've received the revelation.

You've discovered the divine power within.

Now go—

Finish well.

The earth is groaning...

The Spirit is hovering...

The heavens are watching...

And you, dear reader, are the one we've been waiting for.

The 48 Laws of Divine Power are now yours.

Walk in them.

Live by them.

Finish with them.

Now, live like someone who has seen the face of God...

Because you have, because that same Spirit that raised Christ from the dead, now lives in you.

Amen.

ACKNOWLEDGMENTS

Before one law was ever written, before one chapter ever took shape, there was grace.

I must first thank God, not just for the gift of divine power, but for the patience He showed when I questioned whether He called the wrong man. Because I've made missteps. My past isn't polished. There were moments when I wondered, *What if the naysayers dig up some dirt?* But He reminded me: *Their hands are dirty, too.* We've all missed the mark, but His mercy reroutes, His sovereignty redirects, and His Spirit still sends us forward.

To Him, I give praise for the calling of fatherhood—for my daughters and my son, each one stretching my soul and swelling my heart in distinct ways. I thank Him for grandfatherhood, where I've seen traits passed down through bloodlines and blessings, even unknowingly. As it is in the physical, so it is in the spiritual—we transmit both treasures and trauma. God, thank You for teaching me to steward both.

I'm grateful for husbandhood, a high and holy calling, one that constantly reminds me of Christ's sacrificial love for the

Bride. To love unconditionally, even when misunderstood—that's divine. That's covenant.

I preached my first sermon on November 7, 1990, but it never would have happened had it not been for the late Dr. Dewitt Roland, who gave me a chance. And not long after, Deacon Lonnie Woodberry, my Sunday School teacher, discerned something deeper. At just twenty-four years old, he handed me the helm of his class, then asked with wide-eyed wonder, "So…you put that lesson together like that? No seminary? No theology school?" I told him no, no schooling, and he said, "This is a gift." I didn't know whether to believe him, but he saw something in me I hadn't yet seen in myself.

I want to give honor to Reverend Kenneth West, Pastor Roland's successor, who, rather than exiling me in the shadows, simply met me man-to-man and released me with dignity. He asked if I wanted a letter. I didn't even know what "a letter" was in church vernacular, but I honored his words and quietly left. I didn't know where I would land.

But purpose has a homing device.

I visited a church, joined, and once again had to prove the call—without credentials or paperwork—just by walking in what God gave me. Within time, I was preaching Sunday services and was trusted to lead. Pastor James Coats affirmed what Lonnie had said: that I was gifted to teach and, before long, appointed me as director of Christian education, ordained me, and for a decade I preached, taught, baptized, married, and eulogized—while simultaneously enduring the rigors of medical school and residency.

To those who misunderstood me in that season: I hold no bitterness. Perhaps the optics were off as my priorities were brought into question, but the oil was still flowing. I never lost sight of my calling. I was not sitting down on ministry while seeking medicine. The way I am wired from above, those two were to intertwine synergistically. I assumed that vision and position would be obvious to all, but soon learned God gave me eyes to see that call, but didn't call everyone to see it. So, I pardoned the judgments, and now…here we are. I can only say thank you for your part in keeping me humble…and all the more focused.

I then served with Pastor Gary Agee for several years and realized through every appointment, every transition, every exile, and every elevation—man may make plans, but God orders steps.

To my critics, thank you. To those who said, "He needs to sit down…" or "He just wants clicks," or "He's doing too much," I say, "May the clicks be the cadence you are hearing of my calling confirming God's commissioning." Even your commentary served a divine purpose. To my friends—those who nudged me with messages saying, "Stop playing and write the book"—you may have casually spoken it, but Heaven recorded it, and I responded.

And lastly, to you, dear reader. You could've chosen any other book, any other voice. But right now, at this moment in time, you're reading mine.

And that, my friends? That means everything.

ABOUT THE AUTHOR

DR. CURTIS E. BALL is a physician, minister, and messenger with a singular mission: to bring out the best in people—body, mind, and soul. For more than two decades, he has blended medicine and ministry into a calling that meets people where they are and points them toward wholeness.

As a board-certified physician, Dr. Ball has walked with patients through life's most fragile moments. As a minister, he has preached and taught the timeless truths of Scripture. As an author, he writes with a rhythmic cadence that stirs both heart and mind, making profound truths accessible and alive.

His passion for transformation extends beyond the page. Through webinars, seminars, and faith-based health initiatives, he equips communities to reclaim their health and hope. Through music and lyrics, he infuses wellness with creativity, using sound and story to inspire change.

Whether in the hospital, the pulpit, the classroom, or through the written word, Dr. Ball's life is a testimony of service—an offering dedicated to God and to the uplift of others. His desire is simple yet profound: that every person he encounters would walk away strengthened, enlightened, and encouraged to live at their highest potential.

www.ingramcontent.com/pod-product-compliance
Lightning Source LLC
Chambersburg PA
CBHW030516080526
44586CB00011B/215